D1292115

FACING THE TRUTH

FACING THE TRUTH

by

Martin D'Arcy, S.J.

Dimension Books

Denville, New Jersey

First American Edition 1969
by Dimension Books, Inc

TABLE OF CONTENTS

Facing The Truth
by Martin D'Arcy

PREFACE

The titles of the chapters in this book are so varied that some might suspect the essays were put together in a haphazard way. This is not so, for they bear upon the discussions and controversies which have been current since the Second Vatican Council.

Many changes have taken place since the closing of the Council, and sometimes an appeal made to the Council has a justification for new views which have disconcerted many. In fact most of the so-called catechisms of the Council which looked new were already in circulation before it was called by Pope John XXIII. The work of the Council (as I explain later) was to confirm the traditional and the orthodox, to develop and bring them up-to-date and to present the revealed word of God in a way which the modern world could understand and appreciate. Each age emphasizes an aspect of the good news of Christ, and each age can overstress one of these aspects and tend to neglect others. Each age, again, is to some extent influenced by the social and philosophical ideas of the day. Modernism, for instance, which was condemned by St. Pius X feeds upon the contemporary pragmatism in philosophy. A dry-as-dust scholasticism was also a factor working for its popularity. Much of the spiritual literature at the time and for a long while before it has been overmuch concerned with what I may call the outlook of the diaspora. (I call it the diaspora though others unfairly call it the ghetto.) The Reformation had revealed such slackness and worldliness that the leaders in the church called for a penitential season, an abstention from the world and a life of self-abnegation. The aberrations of certain mystics of the seventeenth century led to a still stronger insistence on virtuous conduct and on the pieties as opposed to contemplation. Hence a period followed marked by heroic asceticism and a denial of any form of humanism, a period which lasted until the beginning of the twentieth century, and called by Maritain "one of spiritual asceticism." Actual grace was taught almost to the exclusion of sanctifying grace — a bad habit possibly due to the famous battle of Dominicans and Jesuits on the problems of grace and free will. As these orders were preeminent in theology, each spent so much time on actual grace and in proving that it was right that no time was left to speak on sanctifying grace and the supernatural life.

There were signs, however, of change before the Second Vatican Council. Books began to appear on the Mystical Body and the supernatural life of the individual in Christ and on the place of the Eucharist in this life both as sacrifice and sacrament. Moreover the immense growth of knowledge, both of nature and of man, inevitably made Christians have a wider interest in the world around them and in the hitherto unknown peoples of the earth and in society. Was the

Christian to continue so withdrawn from all these that it would be dangerous for him to partake in affairs of the world? Was he to follow the advice of a Kempis to return to his cell whenever he could? Again, the notions of historical developments and of liberties raised problems about the development of doctrine itself and of liberty of conscience. Many of us had put forward views on these and related subjects before the Council. Outstanding have been the writings of P. Teilhard de Chardin partly because of their timeliness and relevance to the problems weighing upon Catholics.

Among these problems I have selected a few which have caused much discussion and controversy: the ground of authority, the place of conscience, the mystery of the mass and the real presence, what is meant by the natural law, the relation of man's natural perfection to the divine life bestowed upon him by grace. Of God himself there are theologians who echo Nicholas of Cusa in saying our knowledge of him is no better than a *docta ignorantia.* On the other hand a movement which began with Pierre Rousselot introduces love into the highest philosophic concepts and this line of thought may help us to understand how God can be immutable and yet a real lover of his creatures. Again, it is a truth no Catholic will question that Jesus Christ was both God and man. But the mysteries of his human mind and will are always open to a better understanding and it is in keeping with the spirit of the recent Council that I put forward a tentative hypothesis. Herewith is the interconnection between the essays in this book: they are concerned with subjects arising out of the Council, and which are being debated. Please God they may in a small way make a contribution to our knowledge and love of the *Mysterium Fidei.*

Martin D'Arcy, S.J.

ON CONSCIENCE

Included in a well-chosen anthology from the B.B.C. Radio called *Good Talk* are Mr. Anthony Kenny's reflections on Robert Bolt's play *A Man for All Seasons.* So successful has this play been both on the stage and when filmed that St. Thomas More has become celebrated as one who died for conscience's sake. Bolt makes More take this role: "In matters of conscience the loyal subject is more bounden to be loyal to his conscience than to any other thing. . .A man's soul is his self." That in a certain sense More is the martyr for conscience and so an exemplar for future generations is undoubted. Mr. Kenny, however, takes exception to Bolt's presentation of him. More may have appeared to be a forerunner of modern ideals of toleration and to have foreshadowed the view later developed by Emmanuel Kant. This, however, is to misunderstand the thought of More and the position he took up. Mr. Kenny says that he was only following the medieval doctrine of St. Thomas Aquinas, one which was still prevalent in More's day. How different this was from the kind of conscience emphasized in the play had best be explained in Kenny's own words: "For Aquinas, unlike Kant, the human conscience was not a law giver. Rather a man's conscience was his opinion, true or false, about the law made by God. To act against one's conscience was always wrong because it involved acting against what one believed to be the law of God. But to act in accordance with one's conscience was not always right; for one's conscience might be an erroneous opinion. An erroneous opinion would not excuse a man from wrongdoing, if he acted against a clear law of God. He should have formed his conscience correctly." In forming his conscience a man did not commit himself, to use a modern expression, by choosing and taking a risk or creating his own law. He had to find out from the "wise men" or the scriptures or the unerring voice of Christendom. If he did not do that and trusted what he called his conscience, he was not free from blame. If among the wise there were two sides and they were not of one mind, then and only then could a man choose virtuously, though perhaps wrongly.

On this view the important point is that one should take all means to find out the truth. This is where the divergence shows itself in the More whom Bolt portrays. Bolt's More says to Norfolk: "What matters to me is not whether it's true or not, but that I believe it to be true, or rather not that I *believe* it, but that *I* believe it." The More of history would have answered that he had to act according to God's law, and God's law lay not in the chance decision of a king, even when supported by Parliament, for as he said: "If there were no one but myself upon my side and the whole Parliament upon the other, I would be sore afraid, but, I am not bounden to change my conscience and conform it to the council of one realm against the general council of Christendom."

If Mr. Kenny be right, there is then a serious difference in the interpretation of conscience, and what now is often looked upon as the final judge in moral matters (that is, one's conscience) has by no means behind it all the centuries of Catholic thinking.

But first the claim that More was following the prevalent view of his time must be settled. This prevalent view, we are told, was that held by St. Thomas Aquinas. We have fortunately in short form but very clearly exposed the views of St. Thomas in a book called *Conscience and its Right to Freedom* by the Rev. Eric D'Arcy. In this book the texts of St. Thomas as they appear in his chief works are examined. The first texts are from the *Commentary on the Sentences* where St. Thomas tries to bring consistency and good sense out of his predecessors, who wrote on conscience and had differed as to whether it was a faculty or a disposition or an act, and what St. Jerome could have meant when he wrote that there is a "spark of conscience which was not quenched even in the heart of Cain, when he was driven out of paradise." One thing St. Thomas did establish to his satisfaction — viz., that conscience is a judgment of a kind on a particular act or episode. In the *De Veritate* he returns to the subject, but does not make much advance. In the mature *Summa Theologica*, however, his ideas begin to fall into shape. By synderesis, a term which had caused bother ever since St. Jerome imported it into Christian morals, he says, must be meant those primary principles of morals which are, so to say, engraved in the human mind so as to form a

preconceptional disposition or habit. Conscience itself is an act, a reasonable act, wherein we see what
ought to be done by us. In that respect it can be
called a legislative act, but it is not judicial in the
modern sense except in our judgment about the nature of the act *after* it has been committed. As Eric
D'Arcy tells us this rather uncombed theory of conscience was taken over by his followers (it would have
been fairly well known in the time of St. Thomas
More and has been the official teaching of Thomists
to the present time). He quotes M. Prummer as giving
a resumè of it. "Natural Law denotes the principles
themselves (of morality), the universal principles of
the law; synderesis the habitual grasp of them; conscience, an application, after the fashion of a conclusion of the Natural Law to something which should
be done."

On the content of morals, that is to say, the
binding precepts and their affiliated directives, St.
Thomas has less to say, and as a result, perhaps, there
has been a belt of uncertainty in this region. Some
Catholic moralists, when pressed, fall back on an ultimate principle such as "good must be done and evil
avoided." This sounds like such a dreary platitude
that it appears unhelpful and of no service as a major
premise in the practical syllogism which is supposed
by many to be the proper way of arriving at a judgment on a particular matter. But it is far more likely
that it corresponds with what in logic would be the
function of the principle of contradiction: that is to
say, it controls all moral thinking. Just as A says to B:
"but that won't do, for you are contradicting your-
self," so in morals A says to B: "but you are really

saying that there is no distinction between good and evil" or "your view is an apotheosis of evil." In the *Summa Theologica* St. Thomas says that synderesis provides the first principles of nature and human conduct and he grounds them on what he calls our natural inclinations. This surely is a view of the greatest value, and often forgotten. We tend to search for truths in the field of morals as if we were examining a specimen object, a thing instead of a free human being with desires. We ignore what the attribute "good" means while we try to find out what is self-evident and true for all occasions. These natural inclinations are divided under three aspects of human activity. First man as a subsisting self seeks self-preservation or realization, his well-being; secondly, as an animal he seeks sexual intercourse and therewith family life and the rearing of children; and thirdly, as rational he seeks truth, truth about God, about society and about nature. This does open out on a world in which there are priorities and where duties follow on duties. It leaves us, however, still groping for certainties of the kind like those which can be found in the strict sciences and in portions of philosophy. Aristotle maintained that it was a mistake to look for such certainties where by the nature of the subject matter they could not be found. A human being is distinct by possessing liberty of choice and in having to deal with ever changing situations. St. Thomas is in agreement with him in so far as he favors deductive argument less than a rational reflection on our natural inclinations. Just as we use grammar and syntax correctly without sweat of brow, similarly in morals with the dominant inclinations of our nature. They 'swim'

13

into our ken normally enabling us to see what is to be done and what avoided. (This on a higher intellectual level corresponds with the spontaneous blinking of the eye when danger threatens it, or as our interest spontaneously grows when we start to read what proves to be a poem or novel of quality. In matters halfway between instincts and reasoned processes there are the skills which make for genius in games.) This art of seeing what is relevant varies, and this fact would put us back into serious uncertainty, were it not that both Aristotle and St. Thomas said that difficult cases should be referred to the wise, the *Phronimoi* in the Greek, the *Prudentes* in the Latin. This is where Anthony Kenny finds a sharp difference between the Thomas More of history and the hero of Bolt's play. Bolt makes conscience stand by itself, whereas More's conscience was well informed; he abides by God's law and "the general Council of Christendom." His "indictment is grounded upon an Act of Parliament directly repugnant to the laws of God and his holy Church . . ."

But this is perhaps to simplify a problem where arguments could be used for both sides. St. Thomas in some places uses language which seems to limit a certain and clear conscience to what should be obvious as he thinks, to any person and to what has been handed down from Revelation. When it comes to stating what is obvious, he is not sufficiently explicit and he seems not at ease when a person has what is called an erroneous conscience. He taught as most moralists have taught that the object of the will is the good, not as it is in itself but as it is presented by the reason. This does not mean he favors subjectivism in morals. He recognizes the well-known fact that the good appears in different ways and makes an individual appeal, despite the truth that human beings all have the same ends. The result of this is that the will may be mistaken. If a man steals from another in the belief that money should be distributed equally, he is doing what is evil but with, it is assumed, a good conscience. Hence a problem. Pseudo-Dionysius laid it down that "perfection comes only from a total cause; let one point be missing and the whole is bad." Therefore a man must follow his conscience, and in doing so does right, but in choosing a wrong action he commits evil. Whatever he does, apparently, he must be doing wrong. So little were the subjective rights of a man reflected upon at the time that moralists were unwilling to excuse a man who does wrong merely because he believes that he is doing right. In most of his discussions on conscience St. Thomas states that "a man who follows an erroneous conscience is not exempt from sin." In another place he stops halfway: "where there is such ignorance that a man is in no way to blame for this ignorance itself, he is wholly free from blame." This might look as if he had completely changed. The words, however, are carefully chosen — where the ignorance itself is not blameworthy; and what he means is made clearer when he accepts "what concerns sound morals or the truths of the faith." He modifies these views a little in his later work and he makes a distinction between fact and law. "Ignorance of fact" may be excusable, but not ignorance of law. He is here thinking of an excusable accident and distinguishes it from the laws engraved in the human heart or known from Revelation.

To Father Eric D'Arcy these conclusions of St. Thomas seemed to have in them a promise for a satisfactory view of full freedom of conscience even though as they stand, they are incomplete and inconsistent. Modern Catholic moralists are in agreement with him in defending this freedom, despite protests from conservative thinkers. These latter used to argue that "error has no rights." He quotes well-known moralists such as Genicot and Vermersch who hold that "an erroneous conscience, provided it be certain, shows a man what is God's will for him in exactly the same way as does a correct one" (Genicot, *Institutiones Theologicae Moralis,* Vol. I, p. 42). But does this modern tolerance tally with the real view of St. Thomas More or Bolt's version or with neither? In the quotation from Genicot the clause "provided it be certain," introduces an important though questionable condition. If "certain" means an informed conscience, one that is based on precepts engraved in the mind or on the judgment of the wise or on divine Revelation, the teaching is more or less in agreement with what Aquinas would have held. On the other hand if "certainty" here means that incorrigible subjective belief or conviction, which a man holds passionately, his conscience will as often as not be uninformed and run counter to the judgment of the wise. In both cases, I suppose, we are nearer to what is now accepted as inculpable and tolerated if there be no harm inflicted on the community. The conscientious objector to war sometimes relies on strong feeling against any use of violence or force. Again the Russian troops who invaded Prague were some of them convinced that they were saviors of Czechoslovakia.

They could not be persuaded of the contrary. Many other examples could be given of a certainty which is based on invincible ignorance, but nevertheless is unhesitating. Men and women have given their lives for such beliefs.

Modern Catholic and non-Catholic moralists have decided that such persons also must be allowed their freedom unless it is so against the public good as to be dangerous. But except for the invincible ignorance of the simple on matters outside their knowledge, can they be said to be inculpable? Are the actions which follow on such an erroneous conscience good? As we have seen, St. Thomas liked to call such a conscience an opinionated one rather than a certain one. Where there is only opinion, and there can be only opinion because the information for certainty is lacking, have they not a duty to abide by the ruling of the wise or the State or of the Church or the voice of Christendom? And if they do not do this, can they be called exempt from blame? Could for instance the English Catholics in the time of Queen Elizabeth I have conscientiously refused to obey Pope Pius V when he used his supposed deposing power to end their loyalty to their Sovereign? Cardinal Newman in his *Letter to the Duke of Norfolk* indicates that conscientiously they could resist such a Papal Ordinance. But when Rome would not give them leave to attend Protestant Churches they did, so far as is known, accept in great numbers this extremely hard prohibition, though many must have protested in their hearts against it. This refusal to allow a mere putting in of an appearance in a Protestant Church meant the steady loss of their fortune material and social. It would have been easy and very tempting to refuse and to make this a matter of conscience.

Newman, as mentioned above, cites this example of attending Protestant services. He holds it would "violate our duty to our faith: I should obey the Pope and not the law." He then gives a case where the Pope might not be obeyed, one as relevant today as yesterday. "Were I actually a soldier or sailor in her Majesty's service, and sent to take part in a war which I could not in my conscience see to be unjust, and should the Pope suddenly bid all Catholic soldiers and sailors to retire from the service, here again, taking the advice of others as best I could, I should not obey him." What many would like to see now is a condemnation by the Pope of all war. If that happened, what would an American have to do, when his country was engaged in what he considered a "just war?" Or a Czechoslovakian citizen if his country decided to fight for its life? Now in these cases what do we mean by conscience? Which of the two Mores — Bolt's or Kenny's — is making decisions? In the cases just mentioned and in many others, which are called cases of conscience, strict certainty is absent. At best one could say that there is strong probability. More often when persons refer to conscience they mean an opinion so hotted-up that it becomes incandescent; what S. T. Coleridge calls "Phlogiston in the heart." Some vivid story of injustice, which caused great suffering, turns a man or woman against any system of government which is capitalist. Similarly stories of bombings and massacres can turn one into a pacifist. Conscience here is based on a vivid sense of evil to be avoided or good to be done. More and more is the word con-

science used for a state of feeling aroused by inci-
dents or conditions which stir the moral sense. Where
emotion strikes fire, what is called the practical judgment, based on reason and fortified by the support of
a high tradition, hardly seems to deserve the name
reserved for conscience.

If we consult Newman, we appear to leave the
practical reason behind and to be nearing the voice of
God speaking in and through conscience. Some have
thought that Newman had an exceptional consciousness of God's presence — God and the self were
for him the two most striking self-evident truths —
and the wall of partition between God's voice and his
awareness was unusually thin. For this reason he may
not represent the common denominator of human
conscience. Furthermore he must have learnt in his
education the views of Locke and Bishop Butler. But
that does not mean he would side with Bolt and make
conscience a kind of soul — expression, an existential
commitment and nothing else. In answering Mr. Gladstone's question, how can a Catholic obey two sover-
eigns, the Queen and the Pope, he answered, if ever
this double allegiance pulled him "in contrary ways
then I should look to see what theologians could do
for me, what the Bishops and Clergy around me; what
friends whom I revered." This is in the manner of St.
Thomas More. The concluding words, however, are
these: "If after all I could not take their view of the
matter, then I must rule myself by my own judgment
and my own conscience."

Newman, as other remarks of his make clear,
had others less Christian than Gladstone in mind, ag-
nostics for example, in what he was writing. "All

through my day," he writes, "there has been a reso-
lute warfare against the rights of conscience as I have
described it." The agnostic mind put conscience aside
because "its dictate is an imagination," and "the very
notion of guiltiness, which that dictate enforces is
simply irrational. . ." In the popular mind "the old
true Catholic meaning of the word" can no longer be
found. Conscience is identified with a freedom of
conscience which prefers "to ignore a Lawgiver and
Judge" and "be independent of unseen obligations."
"Conscience is a stern monitor but in this century it
has been suspended by a counterfeit, which the eigh-
teen centuries prior to it never heard of, and could
not have mistaken for it, if they had. It is the right of
self-will."

Against this prevalent misconception Newman
sets what he regards as the true traditional Christian
view, "that universal sense of right and wrong, the
consciousness of transgression, the pangs of guilt and
the dread of retribution. These are the first principles
deeply lodged in the heart of man." What is of natural law is borne up by Revelation, and the Pope has
guard over this heritage of man. Lest it be thought
that the ecclesiastical power, and principally the
Pope, has tried to turn the moral law to its own advantage, Newman goes on to express more fully the
claims of conscience. It is, first, a dutiful obedience
to what claims to be a divine voice, speaking within
us. It is not concerned with speculative truth for it
bears immediately on conduct. He quotes St. Thomas
Aquinas to the effect that it is a practical judgment
"by which we judge what here and now is to be done. "
A collision between it and the Pope's authority is

possible "only when the Pope legislates or gives particular orders. . ." The Pope is not infallible in his orders, no more than St. Peter was when St. Paul withstood him at Antioch. Newman then runs through history giving other examples of Papal mistakes.

Having said this Newman feels the need of making even more clear what he means by conscience. If it has the right to oppose the supreme authority of the Pope when the Pope is judged to be mistaken by conscience, that decision of conscience must "follow upon serious thought, prayer and all available means of arriving at a right judgment on the matter in question." The *onus probandi* lies with conscience, for our first inclination should be to obey. "Prima facie it is his bounden duty, even from a sentiment of loyalty, to believe the Pope right and act accordingly." All self-will must be put aside, everything must be discarded which would distract the will from making an unprejudiced and well-informed decision. How strict Newman was in his own life and in his advice is shown in a letter (quoted in *The Tablet*, 28th September 1968, p. 968) to a Catholic parent who asked if her son should go to Oxford in spite of the Rescript from Rome which sought to dissuade Catholics from going to Oxford and Cambridge (This was revoked after the death of Pius IX). The letter was written before 1870, before that is, the infallibility of the Pope was defined. Nevertheless he replies that "whether the Pope be infallible or not, in any pronouncement he is to be obeyed. . . His facts and his warning may be all wrong. His deliberations may have been biased. He may have been misled. Imperiousness and craft, tyranny and cruelty may be patent in the conduct of his advisers and instruments. But when he speaks formally and authoritatively, he speaks as Our Lord would have him speak, and all these imperfections and sins of individuals are overruled for that result which Our Lord intends. . ." He is convinced that "a blessing goes with it (the Pope's word) and no blessing with disobedience." The same writer to *The Tablet* (Mr. Michael G. Murphy) quotes another passage in a similar vein taken from *An Essay on the Development of Christian Doctrine*. I quote a part of one sentence: "obedience to an ecclesiastical superior may subserve our growth in illumination and sanctity, even though he should command what is extreme or inexpedient, or teach what is external to his legitimate province."

These are hard words for those who press so loudly for rights and the liberty of conscience. I think of the decision by a Pope concerning the adoption by Jesuits and others of many of the customs and rites prevalent in China. The Jesuits were meeting with success, but they were told to give up the practice. The result was the near extermination of the Catholic religion in China, and too late, to judge by human standards, the earlier decision was reversed only after two or more centuries by Pope Pius XI. Newman had himself a very tender conscience, and as I have said, he seems to have had, like St. Augustine, a special consciousness of the presence and will of God working within that conscience. That seems to make him belong to both camps. The oft-quoted sentence from the same *Letter to the Duke of Norfolk* gives an absolute warranty to Conscience: "If I am obliged to

bring religion into after-dinner toasts. . .I shall drink
– to the Pope, if you please – still to conscience first,
and to the Pope afterwards." One has to read this last
statement in the context of his general view. That
view he believed to be the accepted Catholic one, for
he took trouble, after the analysis of conscience
quoted above, to cite the Fourth Lateran Council, the
moral treatises of the Carmelites of Salamanca (who
claimed the conformity of their views with Sts.
Thomas and Bonaventure, with Cajetan and Vasquez
and a host of others) and contemporary moralists
such as Busenbaum, a Jesuit, Corduba, a Spanish
Franciscan, and Natalis Alexander, a French Domini-
can.

How far is Newman right in claiming that his
view of conscience is the traditional Catholic one? We
have seen that he quotes Catholics who were house-
hold names as moralists, but I wonder whether
Anthony Kenny would agree. Kenny said that in the
Catholic tradition conscience was legislative but not
judicial. The implications of this, if I understand him
right, are that a man cannot fall back on himself and
conscience as a judge. Granted that there are precepts
of the natural law which are immediately evident to
the mind, for the most part a judgment has to be
made by reasoning from more general precepts and
seeing under which the particular solution falls. This
is only possible where uncertainty has forced the conscientious man to consult the wise or Revelation and
the traditional teaching of the Church. Authority
must weigh very heavily here. Newman allows this,
but then at the end does he not proclaim that conscience must have the last (judicial?) word. The ques-

tion arises whether he is not, without knowing it, pleasing both Mores, Bolt's as well as Kenny's, and in doing so he might be developing a more enlightened view of conscience. The Thomist view owes much to Aristotle and borrows what is called the practical syllogism: that is to say we conclude that something must be done because it falls under a general precept. There is an art however in seeing what is relevant here and what irrelevant, an art which Aristotle called Discernment or practical wisdom. St. Thomas called this Prudentia; our word 'prudent' unfortunately has ceased to translate it. Now Newman, also, knew his Aristotle and came more and more to appreciate the importance of Prudence or discrimination not only in matters of conduct, but in many other exercises of understanding. His invention of the illative sense is evidence of this. In the *Grammar of Assent* he tells us that judgment "in all concrete matter is the architectonic faculty; and what may be called the illative sense in ratiocination is one branch of it." When explaining what this sense is we read "that in no class of concrete reasonings, whether in experimental science, historical research, or theology, is there any ultimate test of truth and error in our inferences besides the trustworthiness of the illative sense that gives them its sanction. . ." Another point, made by Newman which is relevant is the unconditional character of a real assent helped out by the illative sense. We just say "true! true" to statements we hear or read, but really do not make them our own until they come home to us. The truth, for example, that we must all die lies sleeping until it springs out at us when a death sentence is passed on us or on one of our dearest friends

by the doctor. There is all the difference in the world
between the notional assent and the real one sharply
perceived and perhaps sharply felt; as much difference as between the behavior of the foolish and the
wise virgins!

In a book called *The Nature of Belief* I made
much of Newman's real assent and the illative sense,
using instead the word 'interpretation' to convey an
activity of the mind which plays a large part in our
knowledge and especially where choice is involved. It
seemed to be the missing link which unites interest
with knowing, love with understanding, and it acts on
a higher plane of the mind than the skills which serve
so successfully in games, in business and in the lower
acts. St. Thomas is aware of what I may loosely call
this faculty, though I do not think he meditated on it
overmuch. When he stated that our criteria for the
good were to be drawn from our natural inclinations,
he pressed a button which authorized and encouraged
the use of the illative sense or interpretation. Can we
not now say that the more personal — "existentialist"
Kenny calls it in one place — element in conscience is
justified and is compatible with the traditional Thomist practical reason, which relies on external evidence
for its assured conclusions?

The safest answer to this question is perhaps to
answer "yes," but only with certain conditions and
reservations. The tendency today is to exalt conscience as if it were not only the final tribunal but the
supremely wise and capable one as well. Newman,
just because of his high spiritual sensitivity is here not
the most obvious of guides. As quotations from his
writings have shown he seems to have belonged to

that rare category of theists such as St. Augustine of Hippo, who, without losing their critical sense, can be confident of God's nearness and instress in conscience. St. Augustine wrote that truth "unveils itself to him who lives well, prays well, studies well." "Everywhere, O truth, dost thou give audience to all who ask counsel of thee. . ." (Conf. X, 11). "Truth is near to all, is eternal to all: it prompts from without, it teaches from within." To such privileged and graced minds there is no exaggeration in speaking of God's commandments being written in our conscience. For the majority of us, however, such a belief can have disastrous results. Newman himself was very careful to stress that conscience should be well-informed, and hence that it should rely on the voice of the Church and of Christendom — what precisely St. Thomas More did; but many have erected conscience, as Anthony Kenny points out, into a judicial tribunal of its own. The next step is to turn conscience into a mysterious power or faculty, which may or may not dispense with the time and labor required to find truth. It creates its own certainty exploiting the interpretative or intuitive power of the mind to grasp the primary precepts in order to serve cases where there is no such intuition possible. St. Thomas implies that normally a human being in matters of conscience has to make up his mind by turning the matter over and over and looking to what the wise, the *phronimoi* have said and are still ready to answer if, his own phronesis being inadequate, he appeals to them. Sometimes after weighing all the pros and cons a man is made aware of the more likely answer and he feels that conscience will back up his decision where there is no authoritive claim for obedience on the opposite side. Where there is, Newman, for example, makes it clear in the letter to a parent which I have already quoted, that he should make a virtue of obedience to authority. But with the ever growing sense of responsibility and personal rights and claims, men and women have been tending more and more to protest in the name of their conscience. Rightly so, where sin is in question, but now there is also the assumption that the decision must always, if possible, be left to the individual person. His conscience is the one and only final tribunal. Workmen strike, students refuse to accept the rules of the University, those summoned to war service tear up their draft cards, pacifists on conscientious grounds are prepared to go to prison rather than fight. The word conscience is made to cover many attitudes, some obviously right, others dubious and others again painfully erroneous. Reason and unreason can both be behind the decisions of one who forms his own conscience in this way and trusts its every dictate. In the old days those in authority gave short shrift to all who rejected what was considered by the community or the Church to be righteous commands or revealed truths. The problem which Father Eric D'Arcy faces in his *Conscience and Its Right to Freedom* had hardly occurred to governors and judges in less sophisticated times. For a man to refuse what was obviously right must mean, they thought, that he had a bad conscience. This stimple belief explains the exclusiveness of "outside the Church, no salvation." Far too high a belief in the rationality of man and his openmindedness to truth! They were less harsh on ignorance of fact, but a law

27

of God or of Revelation must appeal to every honest creature of God. There might be ignorance, of course, and instruction as to the truth required; but if the man remained obdurate, his decision was inexcusable and he deserved to be punished. This was a simple and straight-forward view, built on an unexceptional a priori view of man as a rational animal created by God. It continued to be held despite experience to the contrary until it became obvious that man in other parts of the world differed on what constituted good and bad; the Hindus on the duties of widows, the Moslems on wives, the Incas on human sacrifice. Besides in the wars of religion in Europe such contrary views could be held with intense religious ferocity. This led also to a new questioning of what were the first principles of the Natural Law as it was called, for they have proved more elusive than expected, even though all the great societies, Chinese, Indian, Jewish and Iranian have much in common. But leaving this aside, religious controversies gradually made each party come to realize that the opponent was in good faith and not just possessed by the devil. The change here was slow but momentous. For centuries, for example, the Catholic Church had taken for granted that its teaching was so clear that no one who rejected it could be saved. Now at the latest Council, Vatican II, all are taken to be in such good faith that an Ecumenical movement has been enthusiastically encouraged. Similarly with the Ten Commandments and other precepts, which specify the high ends of human nature; for centuries it was assumed that they could not be broken or denied without sin. Whoever broke them must, therefore, be treated as a wilful sinner. But by the time of St. Thomas this position had already been shaken, though a satisfactory answer was still in the making. Father Eric D'Arcy argues with force that the principle of freedom of conscience, and consequently of toleration, was already implicit in the teaching of St. Thomas. But with the Christian revelation challenging all men by the light of its truth St. Thomas did not draw the rightful conclusion from his premises. A problem also to the medieval moralists, and in our own day, is how a human act can be both good and bad at the same time. A father consumed with compassion for the intense suffering of his little child and soon to die, stops the suffering by ending the life of the child. He is convinced that he has done right. Nevertheless the act is definitely one of murder, a wrong act. The moralists now say that subjectively the act is good, but objectively bad. They go on to say that unless the social order is harmed by an act of this kind, it should be tolerated. We should always give the benefit of the doubt to one with an erroneous conscience. In other words freedom of conscience is always to be respected where the act is not seriously damaging to the social order. I think that now all moralists are agreed on this, and I think this reaction is due to the growth in experience and in human relations, and mutual human respect. At its basis lies the Gospel bidding that we are not to be judges of others' actions and motives. It is far better that, wherever possible, we should give credit to our neighbors' honest intentions. This does not mean, however, that in theory we must think of human beings as ever straining to be sincere and highminded; nor again should we ignore what is becoming better and better understood, the subconscious or unconscious motivation of very many human acts. In the evolution of human manners there is a debit account as well as a credit one. On the credit side is the ever improving appreciation of human dignity and human interdependence. Slavery has been checked, animals have come to be treated with much greater kindness, the sick and the old are looked after, and the belief in freedom has given a new meaning to democracy. Nowadays we are called upon to respect human rights and to increase man's liberties. On the debit side we have learnt a bitter lesson of how violent sadist impulses can become, and as to motivation the discoveries since the advent of Freud are disconcerting. Throughout the discussion of conscience I have taken for granted the old, accepted view of human nature and human motives – that for example, a man can without too much difficulty make up his mind, know where he stands and judge the degree of certainty and truth in what he is saying. To many this is far too optimistic an attitude. Passion and desire can play underground such a persuasive and cogent part in the resolves which conscience poses, that certitude is rare; that rationalization frequently takes the place of reason, and so we do not see the truth through our own fault. So I end by hoping that each will say to himself "Confiteor," admitting his frailty; he ought, at the same time, to believe that his neighbor is, even when gravely mistaken, a sincere person whom God commends.

ON THE VATICAN COUNCIL II

A new sense of unity in a spiritual warfare befits the new age of the Church and of the world. The world has changed with extraordinary rapidity in the last twenty years. Before then we had on one side a number of dominant countries with empires and federalisms; and on the other vast numbers of peoples still subject and gradually approaching maturity and independence. Then the scene changed; two vast powers holding opposite views of life faced each other and innumerable new races and countries were accepted as adult and entered the "United Nations" as equals with the older powers. So now a new world shivers as it sheds swaddling clothes and starts life often without any belief in Providence or a hopeful philosophy. The Church on its side has been sensitive to new movements within it. In what has been called the Counter-Reformation the Church set about curing itself of the worldliness, which had weakened its divine mission, by means of spiritual exercises and a stricter discipline. Its spirituality became austere, athletic and devotional, and it no longer took the lead in culture or science. But with the present crisis in the social, political world and the deep angst which pervades civilization, a new inspiration has come and with it a new current of ideas. The Council has felt the force of this current, and has therefore made decisions which will be far-reaching. But even supposing that the new ideas did not come to a head at the Council, they are like a tide which in the end cannot be resisted.

What then are these ideas which the Council has deliberated and sifted? They are to be found now in essays and periodicals and in the more progressive books which are being published. There are many, and at first sight they may seem varied and disconnected. Nevertheless there is a connection and it is this which I will try to show. The individualistic form of spirituality has gradually ceded its sovereign position to that of a more communal worship. Now as in early days it is the liturgical service of the Mass which stirs the mind – all Catholics, gathered in one body under the Headship of Christ, offering the one redemptive sacrifice of the Cross to the Father. Gathered together, Catholics make up the Mystical Body which is the form His new Covenant took when He was to be seen no longer according to the flesh but to live and in a mysterious way to grow in his members until the day of the Second Coming. The life of the Mystical Body is nourished by the Eucharist and has for its principle sanctifying grace. A generation or so ago few knew much about sanctifying grace and its corresponding term "supernatural life." Grace was thought of as actual, as a help to keeping free from sin and acquiring virtue. Now instead of the moral virtues attention is more fixed on the great virtues of faith – the believing of the good news of eternal life because one sees with "Christ's eyes;" hope, because the Christ, who has conquered sin and death, lives in us and is stronger than the world; and, above all, caritas, agape, the divine love between the Father and the Son now abiding in us because Christ lives in us.

These great doctrines of Christianity make one whole - and when one aspect is seen another comes to the surface; and that is why the current of change grows stronger with time and cannot be damned. At the Council questions for discussion dealt with the liturgy, the perfection of its form and its possible variety to suit different peoples with different tongues. The lay people now as members of the Body of Christ wish to have a greater share in the Great Sacrifice and to speak with one voice. Immediately the problem arises, where is the one voice when many apparently dissident ones are heard. With the advent of almost universal education and the passing of the period when learning was associated with clerks and clerics, "—the clerks of Oxenford—" the laity are asked to take on much of the work outside the strictly sacerdotal, which the clergy in darker days had assumed. A grown up laity is aware of its liberties and sensitive to restrictions which seem more suited to far off times than now. Hence already there are to be found modifications in the discipline of the Church, in its censorship on reading and social relations with other religions. Greater encouragement is being given to leadership in social and political affairs and to the study of the secular sciences and philosophies. Emphasis is being placed rather on what can be done positively for God and neighbor than on the avoidance of sin. Some even express the hope that in time the form of moral theology may be changed with a new governing principle, that of the charity of the New Testament, instead of legal and ethical prin-

ciples drawn partly from the Greeks. As in all movements of change there are wildly novel and ultra-con-
servative ideas bruited abroad. Old heresies are
vaunted as if they were bright new truths and everything that is old is declared out-of-date. A crisis, too,
like the present tends to separate the wheat from the
chaff. The faithful however still rejoice in the promise
of the continuous Presence of the Paraclete, the Spirit
of Truth and the Comforter.

The horizon keeps on widening the more we follow the logic of this new outlook. The old fear of the
"heretic" or unbeliever which created situations of
utter distrust and hate may give way to a dialogue
which would turn reunion from being a faint dream
into a possible reality. Recriminations and bitter disputes could become a thing of the past. (Some, unfortunately, seem to have transferred their recriminations and dislikes to their fellow Catholics, especially
if they hold a position of authority. Enthusiasm
touched up by prejudice can make the eyes of faith
of which St. Augustine spoke, squint). In all such
changes, meetings, and adventures one thing is ever
necessary, and that is a reliance on divine grace and
the power of Christ's Resurrection. And this mention
of Resurrection brings us back to the main theme of
Catholic thought which is developing. The tragedies
of the late Middle Ages turned those sunk in misery
to the consolation of Christ's passion, and since then
prayers and hymns and devotions have harked back
to Gethsemane and Calvary. The greatest spiritual
riches came from such meditations; but in the Pauline
and complete theology of the Church, Calvary and
the Resurrection are never to be taken in isolation

from one another. The Christ of the Mystical Body and of the Mass is the Risen Christ, the source of our faith and hope, and the Lord of life who has conquered death. In this setting all the tendencies which I have mentioned fall into place in the realization, that is, of Christ as Kurios, the Lord, whose victory is final though we must wait till the Second Coming for the consummation to see how and when mankind and the Universe will be Christ's. He will be "all in all" and restore Creation to his Father.

We have to look with new eyes at history and see with new understanding the development of science and the ever richer complexity of this earth and of man's place in it, as well as the firmament of planets and stars; for the larger the Universe reveals itself, the closer to our own life's ideal it comes. A hundred years ago a view such as that expressed by P. Teilhard de Chardin could never have been understood or tolerated. Now despite the imperfections from which it suffers it fits the vision now dawning before our eyes, the vision of Christ as the Alpha and Omega — as the Lord who brings order and meaning into the world; as the Son of God and Son of Man who by the Cross destroys sin and death; and by his resurrection and in the Mystical Body is creating a new society which is better than any new superior species in that it is both human and divine.

ON AUTHORITY

In The Times of London, November 9th 1968, a Mr. John Skinner wrote an article entitled *The Roman Church Crisis on Authority*. It was devoted to a criticism and correction of the Church's view today. He claimed it was and is against the Biblical tradition. The Jews' "need for law came not from God, but from their own failing weakness." "The transparent authority of God's truth speaks direct to conscience." "Christ," he assures us, "did not found his authority upon law, but on the truth of his own words, . . . his gospel proclaimed freedom from the law." "The New Testament word for authority, it has been said, is best translated by competence in the sense that we talk of a doctor as competent in the field of medicine. Thus the leaders of the People of God do not take their authority from some legal, quasipolitical power but from the charisma of Christ, that marks them off as the competent servants of the Gospel."

The substitution of medical competence for divine authority might seem ridiculous, were it not backed up in a less extreme manner by some scholars in recent times. Today and yesterday we have been witnessing an antipathy to the very word authority. It does not fit in with the liberal creed which would oust the old Christian one. In his *Grammar of Politics*, for instance, the late Harold Lasky confessed he could find no meaning in the term sovereignty, and he has had many followers. More surprising is it that such a distinguished philosopher and Anglo- Catholic as A. E. Taylor should belong to the same camp. In his Gifford Lectures *The Faith of a Moralist* he expresses his agreement with another Christian philosopher, W. G. de Burgh: "As W. G. de Burgh says '*Auctoritas*' means moral influence; the English word authority in the sense of executive power would be expressed in Latin by *imperium* or *potestas*.," There is no doubt truth in this, but it has a suggestio falsi as if the two words were unconnected, whereas historically and naturally in time the one word *auctoritas* was used to cover both meanings. This was eminently suitable when God's word was enunciated. It had truth and power behind it. Before even his conversion Newman foresaw the danger to religion of the liberal spirit which was spreading fast. As it took shape it's advocates grew more and more irritated by the inflexible attitude of the Catholic Church, and sought for grounds for their belief elsewhere than in the authority of God. By 1870 Pusey complained that in the Anglican Church "instead of one Phaeton there have been 30 or 300: each guiding the chariot of the sun after his own fashion." Composite books, *Essays and Reviews* in 1860 and *Lux Mundi* in 1889, *Foundations* and *Essays Catholic and Critical* in 1926 marked the steady drift away from the old idea of authority. *Auctoritas* is translated as "corporate witness" or "inspired witness." Disliking what was called the oracular conception of the Catholic Church, and forsaking the old unquestioned authority of the Bible, Protestant writers were hard put to it to go beyond "private conscience" or "adherence to Christ himself." So liberal and permissive has Church or Civil society become that many in despair in Germany, Italy and Russia were willing to conjure up a devil in order to restore law and order.

This decline in authority has been made responsible for much of the indiscipline and disorder in private and civil life. A fixed belief, with sanctions, it is claimed, is necessary for the well-being of man. He cannot do without laws, law courts and prisons of one kind or another. Human nature works when there is a known ultimate tribunal and rules which are accepted and obeyed without reflection. What a fixed standard such as gold is to exchange and barter, such is a certain and definite code of belief in the moral order. Deprived of a firm religious authority which draws back the curtains of eternity, moral beliefs are left at the mercy of passing fashions, and as "bad money drives out good" so irregularities increase and evil practices come to be tolerated and then accepted. On the other hand a divine authority keeps before man's eyes the majesty and purity of God and so raises the level of conduct. It reminds man both of the summit of perfection he can attain by arduous effort and divine grace and points starkly to the ruin and suffering evil brings in its train. Those with a knowledge of history are well aware of this. Here a Pope and an Ortega y Gasset, to take an example, speak with one voice; the latter saying that "without a spiritual power, without someone to command - and in proportion as this is lacking - chaos reigns over mankind;" and Pope Leo XIII in his Encyclical *Libertas*: "Of its very nature then and considered from any angle whatever, in individuals or societies, in superiors no less than in subordinates, human liberty implies the necessity of obedience to a supreme, eternal rule, which is no other than the authority of God in his commandments or prohibitions to us."

When then it is suggested by Laski, that the word 'sovereignty' is meaningless, and when Taylor and de Burgh try to rid it of all association with power or sanctions, they are blowing their tobacco smoke into a contrary wind. Least plausible of all is Mr. Skinner when he tries to equate authority with competence. He says he is thinking of the competence, say, of a good doctor. Now let us grant that this is one of its meanings which follows from the primordial meaning as given by the Oxford Dictionary: "the power or right to enforce obedience." But when he denies this original meaning as Biblical and would replace it with 'competence' he makes havoc of holy Scripture. In all societies, civil as well as religious, "the power or right to enforce obedience" is indispensable. Only tiny groups like the Quakers can manage without it. In the Bible God is always exercising authority over a primitive and stubborn people. The authority issuing from Mount Sinai and the Ten Commandments were not treated by the Israelites as merely the words of a competent doctor. God's authority is paramount in the Old Testament, as Newman recognized in one of his sermons on *Subjects of the Day*, preached in 1842 before he became a Catholic.

He took as the title of his sermon *The Christian Church an Imperial Power*, a provocative title, and one he proved by an impressive succession of texts from David and the Psalmists and Isaiah. Let one suffice: "It shall come to pass in the last days, that the mountains of the Lord's house shall be established in the tops of the mountains ... and He shall judge among the nations and shall rebuke many people." In the New Testament the note of Kingship holds pride of place. Out of Bethlehem "shall He come forth unto me, that is to be the ruler in Israel." The first words of Christ in His public ministry and the last concerned His Kingdom. Skinner asserts that Christ did not found his authority on law but on the truth of his own words. The Gospel proclaimed freedom from the law. That is why, I suppose, his listeners felt that he was as one who spoke with authority, and why he also taught that he had come not to destroy the law but to fulfill it! It is quite evident that the people came to hear him because they felt the power as well as the truth of what he was saying. The Christ of the Gospels who was so insistent on telling the crowds the will of his heavenly Father is not to be set down as a competent physician. Nor was St. Paul thinking of his competence only when he threatened the sinner in his Letter to the Corinthians; nor lastly St. John in the Apocalypse. He is more like himself "a son of thunder" in his admonitions to the Seven Churches.

Authority, though in its two chief manifestations, i.e. in parents and rulers of States it is easily recognizable, does unfortunately become clouded with doubt when belief in God weakens. The root of authority lies in there being someone responsible for an action with the power also to enforce it. As the Centurion says in the Gospel: "I am a man having authority: I say to this man, come, and he comes; and to this man, go and he goes." The more important the office or man the greater is his authority and the name of 'sovereign' marks the intimate union of supreme office and corresponding power. In any civilized society there are degrees of authority, a parent's towards his children, a minister of health or of defense, and as the purpose of their office is essential for the welfare of others, their authority is moral and the sanctions are moral. All authority ultimately descends from God, and Pope Benedict XV in his Encyclical Letter at the outbreak of the war of 1914 reminded the nations of this awe-inspiring truth: "We remind the peoples of the earth of that doctrine which no human opinions can change: There is no power but from God; and those that are, are ordained of God. Whatever power then is exercised amongst men, whether that of the King or that of an inferior authority, it has its origin from God." This ultimate sanction - I may add, sanctification - has given that quasi-mystic sense to those who are God's anointed, whether Bishop or King. Once this Christian ideal weakens, all authority begins to be questioned, and in place of God we have the exaggerated claims of private judgment and democratic vote. "We are like Jeroboam who made his own religion." It is far better and safer to be ruled by God than by public opinion, a dictator or the sayings of a Mao.

But what if, while suffering from the dead hand of legalism and of overbearing authority we set our-

selves to the task of giving all this authoritarianism
the coup de grace and replace it by reliance on the
Holy Spirit heard in the voice of the people of God?
This is the new ideal proposed by the Reverend
Daniel Maguire in Commonweal (November 8, 1968).
He regards the structure of the church as not God
given but rather due to the unfortunate vicissitudes of
history.

With Constantine, for example, special honors
and authority were assumed by Bishops. "Heavily ju-
ridical notions of authority, society and office seeped
into the Christian ecclesial mind. The osmosis of Roman legality was thorough." This led to the glorifica-
tion of Roman law. A further change occurred in the
Middle Ages when Popes sought to turn the church
into a sovereign society. There is no need to unfold
further the pitiful tale of how Popes moved into a
position of complete absolution and the administration of the church hardened into a secular legal system. By the time of Vatican II the "hierarchical mag-
isterium purports to moving amid theological findings
and as though with a divining rod to discern truth
from error." "The inevitably limited witness of de-
ceased Popes is heard with fixational intensity, while
the presence of the spirit in the living church is by-
passed." The only remedy in this account is to return
to the spirit of the Gospels and early church for the
authority to rule cannot be conceived as divinely im-
parted and existing independently of the will of the
community.

Even conservatives would agree, I think, that legality, as seen in the appeal to canon law and in all
the apparatus of administration, has been excessive.

One of the aims of the late Council was to free the church from its time-wasting procedures and regulations. Such a process of spring cleaning is needed in every long-lasting society, even in one which has supernatural origins. But to present the case against the church's legalism and authority as though a new start were needed because the very working of the Holy Spirit had been cut off is conspicuously untrue, as the remarkable evidence of saints among members of the nineteenth century church proves. Moreover it is based on a naturalistic approach backed up by bias for Rousseauist democracy. This naturalistic attitude blinds the writer to the genuine growth of the church through the centuries and the dependence of that growth on Rome's authority, as witnessed in the missionary work of St. Boniface and St. Patrick and their devotion to the vicar of Christ and later the fruitful obedience of martyrs and congregations of religious men and women. St. Francis of Assisi, the most unjuridically minded of men, had unswerving devotion to the Holy See and a story I recommend to Father Maguire is the dream of Pope Innocent III of a poor man holding up the church from falling. Incidentally, the Franciscans would have fallen into anarchy themselves within one generation had it not been for the measures taken on their behalf by the people of authority.

The Gospels do not support Father Maguire. Take one example from the Sermon on the Mount where our Lord says: "That any man who is angry with his brother must answer for it before the court of justice and anyone who says 'Raca' to his brother must answer for it before the council and anyone who says to his brother 'thou fool' must answer for it in hellfire." Here is authority with a vengeance! Ought not, too, the last chapter in the fourth Gospel (perhaps the most moving and beautiful in the New Testament) to be omitted? All too clearly Christ there confers on St. Peter the highest authority, that of the chief shepherd, a biblical title for a king or one with plenipotentiary powers. Bishops and Popes, we are told, have gradually down the ages acquired powers which are alien to the Gospel teaching and spirit. But those who think in this way have forgotten, I fear, the grievous responsibility imposed on those who have to guard God's temple and the purity of divine teaching. God and democracy have little in common. We can speak to a human being as man to man; we should approach God on our knees and even though we are taken into his love, fear and trembling should not be far away. In the prayers of the church the awful majesty of God is always recognized. Now the church knows that this God has deigned to teach through his Son the words of life, words which came straight from the mouth of God himself. It is idle to talk about authority based on any historical developments which put past utterances out of date. We cannot begin to be wise in our judgment about authority and development until we come to realize what it means to have God's truth instead of our own, once and forever spoken. Such words are death-dealing as well as life-giving and those who play fast and loose with them are playing with fire. So seriously has the church always regarded the divine message and so shocking a denial of the ipsissima verba that it may well have acted over-conservatively in its guardianship of them as one might handle delicately and infinitely precious objects or a vital medicine which could destroy mankind it it went into the wrong hands.

THE REAL PRESENCE

The story of the Exodus of Israel from Egypt is one of the most dramatic in literature. It must have appeared strikingly dramatic and illuminating as well to the early Christians. As Jews they knew so well what the feast of the Passover commemorated. The connection between the saving blood on the lintels of the Jewish homes and the blood shed on Calvary for the redemption of the world, the lambs to be sacrificed and the Lamb of God, was vivid and stark. The feast was the most obvious prototype in its close resemblance to the fulfillment in Christ and the Eucharistic sacrifice. Other foreshadowings in the Bible have been pointed out, some recalled by Christ himself, which reveal their full meaning in what is to come. Of such the manna in the desert is, probably, the most obvious, and we have, too, the Shekinah or Divine Presence in the Holy of Holies of the Temple. In the Prologue of the fourth Gospel an intimate connection between this Presence and Jesus Christ, the Word made Flesh, seems suggested by the very choice of words by the Evangelist. The Greek work Eskenosen, meaning tabernacling, or pitching a tent, created by its very sound an association with the Shekinah in the

Temple.

Now this tabernacling — "what dost thou with thy tribe's black tents that hast the red pavilion of my heart?" - leads us straight to a proper understanding of the mysterious mode of God's salvation "through the flesh" and his being with us all days in his Church and in its principal act of worship. Christ claimed to be the Way, the Truth and the Life. In the first part of the Mass we listen to God's word and accept Him as the Truth and his teaching also as the Way. But the second part of the Mass shows Him forth as the living Way. St. Paul tells us that He accepted an obedience which brought him to death, death on a cross. That is why God has raised him to such a height and given him that name which is greater than any other name. The Victim of Calvary risen from the dead becomes the living bread, the Life of the world - "the Lamb," whom St. John saw in vision slain but alive - and it is this sacrificial Lamb who is made present and life-giving in the Sacrifice of the Mass, but in the new form of Presence foretold in the Eucharistic sermon on the hillside across the sea of Galilee. After Our Lord had shown the marks of his wounds to the doubting St. Thomas he said that those who did not see him visibly but believed were to be blessed, implying that the same real risen Christ would be as equally the true object of their belief as the Christ the Apostles could see and touch. They were to be in no real sense worse off because His Presence was no longer to be sensibly experienced.

The Eucharist is the divine stratagem wherein in every age the real Lord, obedient unto death and ex-

alted by the Father could be with his own in an intimacy of Agape. Those who accepted Him would
share His very life, and this sharing would be both
symbolized and realized in the sacrifice and sacrament of the Mass. By the new Covenant time would
not interrupt or bring to an end the formative act of
the whole of history; it, so to speak, repercussed in
every generation allowing those who lived in 1000
A.D. or 1968 to meet Christ as the Way, the Truth
and the Life in all ways the same except that His
Presence would be realized sacramentally and not visibly. This unique prerogative needs special emphasis
today when the very word 'static' has a figurative
sound. Development certainly there must be, but the
development of anything living or of a truth depends
upon a permanent identity in change and consists also
in a deeper understanding of what is so lovable and
profound that any loss of the original would be a
disaster. Those who are oversensitive to what is contemporary are often tempted to compare it favorably
with what has preceded it in time; Hence they seize
upon what is passing, Cartesian ideas or transcen-
dental idealism or pragmatism and social and cultural
fashions and make an idol of them. The Catholic view
of the Eucharist and the doctrines involved in it had
been hammered out and gradually defined, and the
Thomist view of sacrifice and sacrament had come to
be accepted as the best philosophical formulation of
them. The later period of the Middle Ages, however,
saw a decline in faith and morals. The doctrines of
sacrifice and transubstantiation had a tired look, pro-
tected as they were by a cobweb logic. The Reforma-

tion was an attempt to get back to a richer piety and a deeper commitment. To Catholics, however, this reaction was thought to go too far, to empty the baby as well as the water out of the bath. The Real Presence was spiritualized and became ghostly: the consecrated bread and wine of the Eucharist were to be regarded now as symbols of spiritual union with Christ. The Mass was rejected as an attempt to add to the one unique Sacrifice of Calvary. It had begun as a memorial feast or thanksgiving supper and this form of it should be restored. Thus six to eight centuries of Christian life were condemned as mistaken and even as idolatrous. Obviously on such a view the sixteenth century Presence of Christ could not be the same as it had always been; it looked as if the divine stratagem had failed or had never been intended, for the relation of the Christian to the real Christ risen in body and possessed still of flesh and blood, which the Apostles had known was far different from the symbolic one occasioned by a memorial service.

The word 'real' here is the operative one, and the Catholic Church in insisting on the Real Presence means by that the real corporeal Presence of Christ — a presence as real as that which St. Thomas felt and touched, what, to use a Pauline image, wedded persons experience in marriage. Modern Biblical scholarship has done much to justify this tradition by emphasizing the realistic thinking of the Jews. (I should call it 'down-to-earth' were it not that the corporeal and the spiritual come together in their religious thought). It was this realistic attitude which made the Jews, when they heard Our Lord declare that He was the living bread and "whoso eats my flesh and drinks my blood dwells in me and I in him," take for granted that he meant what he said literally though spiritually. Christ did not rebuke them for so doing, nor did He deny that his words were "hard sayings." St. Paul also wrote of the Body of Christ and scholars have been uneasy as to how to interpret him. Is the Body of Christ when used of the Church a collective noun, symbolizing "the unity of the Church with Christ," or has it a realistic visible connotation? Many now lean to the latter view and argue that St. Paul was so alive to the presence of the Risen Christ that he saw it as that which gives life to his followers. They become Christ in a mysterious way as they are made members of the Risen Body - an extension of Christ himself. Pierre Benoit and others have pointed out that the Jews did not speak of the body as an element in the composite, which makes up a human being. Instead they spoke of an animated and corporeal person and hence St. Paul meant by 'body' the whole body-person. He uses also the image of 'head' - which at first designated authority, but in the Letter to the Ephesians (I,22-3) it is combined with the body and later in Ephesians IV,16, and in the Letter to the Colossians II,19, it is equated with the animating principle of the body.

A full understanding of what St. Paul was trying to say may be so linked up with the mystery of the divinity and human nature in Christ and the properties of a human nature glorified and divinized as Christ's was, that it must await our own resurrection of the body. As it is, the apparitions of Our Lord during the 40 days after the Resurrection give evidence that His Risen Body has powers and characteristics not only unexpected but hardly credible. We can infer from these manifestations that what is called the transubstantiation of bread and wine with that Risen Body may be through relationships which are beyond our understanding. We do know that what was ordinary bread and wine is when consecrated the real Body and Blood of Christ, and the word transubstantiation, without any particular philosophical allusion, serves to state the true and real complete change. But with our ignorance of the properties of what is not only a risen body, but one glorified by being hypostatically united to the Godhead, the knowledge will always probably be *docta ignorantia.* The change is certainly not explicable in terms of chemistry or transformation, nor does the term transignification do justice to the corporeal relationship between Christ and His Mystical Body, the Head and the Members.

St. Paul had, so to speak, to twist and torture his vocabulary in order to express this new and startling kind of consanguinity now existing between his converts and the real Jesus whom he preached. One can see a development in his letters and in the way he makes use of terms such as "headship" and "fullness" (pleroma). He was trying to communicate what he held to be the consummation of the Christian life, namely the partaking of the very Body and Blood of Jesus Christ and thereby being privileged to have Him living in their hearts. Baptism, he taught was the beginning of a new kind of life. In its visible rite it symbolizes and signifies the death of the "old man" in us. Both in the Letters to the Romans and to the Colossians entrance to the new life is gained first by

the death of the old life in baptism. "In our baptism
we have been buried with him, died like him" — and
so "we have to be fitted into the pattern of his resurrection as we have been into the pattern of his death"
(Romans VI, 4-6). Clearly the Redemption is seen as
comprising two acts in one drama — and they must be
seen together, if the nature of the drama of Redemption is to be fully understood — the death on Calvary
and the Resurrection from the dead. "If we have died
with Christ, we have faith to believe that we shall
share his life" (Romans VI, 8). In the Colossians after
stating that "in Christ the whole Plenitude of Deity is
embodied and dwells in him, and it is in him that you
find your completion," St. Paul goes on to state that
"you by baptism have been united with his burial,
united too with his resurrection, through your faith
in that exercise of power by which God raised him
from the dead." St. Paul in these exhortations is
playing upon the theme of the analogy of death and
life as achieved by Christ by his death and resurrection. Baptism is unfinished business until it is comple-
ted by the Eucharist. It has been compared to the
espousals which look forward to marriage, and St.
Thomas Aquinas in accordance with St. Paul and the
tradition of the Church teaches that Baptism has
what he calls a votum, that is a pledge of the
Eucharist. A modern comparison would be of a
boarding card for a plane given in virtue of one's
ticket. The completion, which St. Paul writes of, is
the Eucharist for, like consummated marriage, it is a
union in which we become one flesh and one spirit
with Christ himself. Marriage, indeed, is praised by St.
Paul precisely because it is on a lower level a symbol

of the union of Christ with his Church, the loving personal Head with the living personal members. One can see from this how wrongheaded are those who write and speak as if by baptism we gain all that is promised by Christ in the supernatural order. Equally in error are those who would allow the non-Catholic to partake of the Body and Blood of Christ in the Communion of the Mass. That would be as if a stranger could share the marriage bed of a husband and wife, for the intimacy of a Catholic with Christ Our Lord is more intimate and sacred than any other family tie.

All this brings out the nature of the Eucharist as heavenly food. There have been attempts again and again to make of the union of Christ with his members a spiritual union which would be easily intelligible. The explanation then would be that members of the Catholic Church are united with God and graced so as to share His mind and love. The sacramental banquet at the close of the Mass would be symbolic of this union. But this is to underrate all that Holy Scripture has to say on the reality of Christ's living body and blood and the part it plays in uniting us to a Christ living with His risen Body in a union analogous to that of marriage. The true Body and Blood of Christ is the core of the mystery of our Redemption. That is why the Church instinctively as well as logically has held firmly to the real bodily presence of Christ in the Eucharist. Many devotions have sprung from this belief — devotion to the real Presence in Churches, to Perpetual Adoration, to the Sacred Heart, to Corpus Christi processions. The new exclusive passion for the liturgy has cast a shadow

54

over these devotions. But they arise out of the sensus fidelium, spontaneous outbursts of love towards one who became a man for our sakes and saved us through his bodily wounds and death. They need not interfere with or distract persons from the sublime official worship of God in the Eucharist. This is the center and source of man's spiritual life, but there is room for individual and very human approaches to Christ, even as the Apostles and Disciples must have rejoiced in spending loving hours with Him who one day would reign from a cross and so redeem them.

It is right, however, that nothing should distract us from the glory of the Eucharistic Sacrifice. Here is the epitome of our faith, the source of our hope and Christ's crowning act of love. We are brought near to the Cross and by faith we know that we have present on the altar the very Christ who reigned from the Cross — the cosmic and perfect act of our Redemption is not only portrayed; it is exemplified and situated anew wherever the priest consecrates the bread and wine. Without the real presence our worship would be no more than a memorial service, we should not be able to live by the divine life as the new born feed at their mothers' breasts. We have both the symbol and the reality; the symbol lies in the offering of the bread and wine, our offering in reparation and out of love; and the reality the divine Victim given to us by the Father as a token of reconciliation. After the Consecration the priest and the people begin with the words *"nos servi tui, sed et plebs tua sancta"*; servi, that is to say, servants if we look at ourselves before God, but now "thy holy people" because by the New Covenant we are heirs and co-heirs with

Christ, members now of His Risen Body, able to say *Abba Father* at the Pater Noster with Christ's very voice as sharers in the divine nature. Until the end of time Christ grows winning all by His love, and each generation fills up what is wanting for the accomplishment of God's great design, the world submissive and human beings "born anew with an immortal, imperishable birth, through the word of God who lives and abides forever" (St. Peter I Epistle 123-124).

NO GOODBYE TO THE ROMAN CANON

We are now to be free to use in the Mass other Canons besides the ones we have read and recited since childhood. Variety may be a blessing but not because of any serious fault in our present Canon. A distinguished critic has called it "admittedly untidy," and many, I suppose, would agree with this description. Nevertheless, I am sure that one can discover in it a unity and a rich and rewarding one. This unity reveals itself in the light of the Mystical Body — those partaking in the Mass being members of it and sharing in the life of the Head, the risen Christ, both Victim and High Priest.

With this clue the prayers of the Mass are seen to be a concerted action, where the first note struck is of our sinful humanity making its sacrificial offering. It is succeeded by a growing confidence in that the dignity of our human nature has been so graced as to become a partaker of Christ's divinity. From then on the action shows the growing realization of what that means — men who are sinners (*nobis quoque peccatoribus*) becoming aware that they can offer the holiest of sacrifices because they are one with Christ himself. We see the human side from the Confiteor through the offering of wine and water on to the Preface. With the words *sursum corda* the scene changes, for the priest and congregation are initiated into the Sacrifice of the Son of God. The trumpets as it were begin to sound as the Lord draws near. He is not only to adorn our sacrifice by his presence, but to take ours into his, and hence there is a burst of thanksgiving and our voices mingle with the Angels and Archangels, the Powers and Dominations, as we cry out "Holy, Holy, Holy, the heavens and the earth are filled with His Glory."

The first movement in the Canon is to rearrange the worshippers' thoughts and ask Christ to bless and make his own the gifts they have brought and then to put all possible intentions and desires in His hands. The Church comes first and then the Pope and Bishop and all who profess the Catholic faith, especially those present, and those they love who are in need. That done, they have the courage and ambition to ask even the elect who are already in bliss and especially the Mother of God herself and the Apostles and saints to come near and protect our still too human offering. The English translation here does not do justice to the significance of this prayer. It just reads: "We honor Mary, the virgin mother of Jesus; we honor Joseph. . ." The omission of "Mother of God" (genitricis Dei) has offended many, but it is the pointless word honor which hides the significance of the Latin. The offering of the faithful has now reached such cosmic grandeur that the Mother of God and all the saints are engaged in the Sacrifice. We see the apocalyptic vision of St. John coming true.

So great has the *mysterium fidei* become that

58

the worshippers with a new sense of their unworthiness renew their prayers that their offering may be acceptable and that they may be numbered among the flock, the elect of God. At the same time they have the confidence to ask that this same offering of theirs may become the very Body and Blood of Christ — which was the instrument of the world's salvation. Then follows the recitative and then the consecration and eucharistic thanksgiving. The Lord has come as He promised. What was his Shekinah or presence in the Temple is now the identical Victim of Calvary, save that He suffers no more and is one risen from the dead. We too in a mysterious way in offering ourselves offer Christ — and we have the power to do it because we are his heirs, co-heirs, sons of God by adoption as Christ is by right. This union becomes clearer and clearer as the Canon moves to its climax. The first act, however, after the Consecration is to offer once again and with joy the offering which is now "a pure victim, a holy victim, an unspotted victim, the holy bread of eternal life and the chalice of everlasting salvation," a gift which is far superior to that of Abel or Abraham or Melchisedech. Mindful again of the scene in heaven described in the Apocalypse the priest asks that what lies before him on the altar may be carried "by thy holy Angel to thy altar on high in the presence of the divine majesty." These words sound at first obscure but the generality of commentators are in agreement with the simple statement of Joly de Choin that "this angel is Jesus Christ Himself, He is the altar, the sacrificing priest, the mediator and the Victim." Put at greater length: "the angel is no other than Christ Himself" if these words refer to the body and blood of Christ for Christ is "most assuredly the Angel of the Covenant whom on the testimony of the prophet Malachi we wish for." Furthermore, the reference in the same prayer to the 'sublime altar' which is in the presence of the divine majesty, is drawn from the Apocalypse of St. John — and all this passage is to be understood mystically of our mediator Christ Himself, for it is Christ who is the priest who offers the sacrifice which is offered and the golden altar on which the offering is made." (James Gordon Huntley, S.J., 1620 A.D.).

This prayer is made confidently for as the Canon continues there is a note of happiness, one in which the virtues of the 'risen life' predominate, namely faith and hope. It is in this hope that an appeal is made for those who are dead and "rest in the sleep of peace" and even for all the faithful who are present themselves, as well as for those who are absent. They too live in Christ. There is an echo of the *Confiteor* in the *nobis quoque peccatoribus,* "sinners though we be," but now all take their place in fellowship with the Apostles and martyrs and the virgin saints and those we have known and loved and who are now with God.

With this last invocation the Mystical Body, Christ and His members, is seen in its true dimension and the banners of the King *(Vexilla Regis)* in his new kingdom shine out over those who have been redeemed at a great price. This holy people *(plebs tua sancta)* at this moment of the climax of the Mass, realizing what has been done for them and what they have become cry out Abba Father, through Him, with Him and in Him. It is a pity that the English translation spoils the climax by putting 'in Him' in the second place. It is because we are in Christ ("no longer I but Christ lives in me,") that we share the sonship of Christ and ratify it by feeding forthwith upon His Body and Blood. Christ's prayer has been fulfilled; the prayer that "the love wherewith Thou hast loved Me may be in them and I in them."

THE CONSCIOUSNESS OF CHRIST

Great lovers of Jesus Christ — and how many
thousands there have been, saints and mystics! — have
never, so far as I know, ventured to ask him about his
human knowledge, its extent and its limitations. And
yet how much we would like to have even a glimpse
of the truth. In recent years with so much new knowledge of the unconscious and subconscious and mind
processes and of the interpenetration of the spiritual
and the material, the connection of thinking, remem-
bering and feeling with brain processes and glands,
one might have expected to find more fruitful studies
in Christology; but we have not been left much the
wiser. A notable attempt has been made by Karl
Rahner, even though some may find his writings obscure. He points out that the objects in consciousness
arrive in different ways and are noticed differently.
Some stand out and are easily attended to; others
remain in the shadows and need reflection to bring
them out. This happens because there is a shadowy
rim to our conscious thought, a kind of non-objec-
tivized knowledge on the horizon which can be made
into clearer objects by concentration on it. We all
know how various matters lie just below awareness

63

and move into focus as need requires. This is the way in which we learn to increase the contents of our knowledge, our mind opening out more and more, as we grow up, to a totality of possible objects among which we pick and choose. On the strength of this, Rahner concludes that this totality or horizon is never fully grasped, but its reality is assured to us by the corresponding but unquestioned knowledge we have of our own spirituality and freedom. These are our birthrights, the abiding primitive data of our consciousness. They are not discovered as we discover ordinary objects; they are taken for granted, the open sesame with which we start life. It is because they are there that we make of our very ignorance and unknowing a positive condition of all our human understanding. Human knowledge, if it be human, is necessarily a process of overcoming ignorance: it requires also time, opportunities and the exercise of free will.

Turning now to the question of Christ's consciousness, Rahner suggests that his awareness of his divinity was analogous to this free and spiritual condition of ours. It was not in the forefront of consciousness; rather it was like that horizon where what we are is taken for granted. It was a presence, more than a truth before the mind; a permanent condition prior to any conceptual objectivization, and it would make itself present in the steady development of soul and mind. Similarly Christ our Lord who "grew in knowledge and wisdom" grew concomitantly in his realization of his divine sonship. He too, like us, had a history through his own human changing experience. We should think, therefore, of our Lord as passing from stages of ignorance to wisdom, even though, like our freedom and spirituality, he always possessed a ground, an un-objectivized "consciousness of his divinity."

Father John Bligh, in an article in the *Heythrop Journal* (Oct. 1968), approaches the same problem from a different angle. He raises the question whether in any sense of the word "faith," our Lord lived by faith and not by sight. In other words, in what way could a human finite consciousness be aware of an infinite divine personality? He distinguishes between the faith possessed by the Apostles, specifically St. Thomas, and our faith. We today have not seen, but we believe: St. Thomas had seen and after the Resurrection he was asked to believe. Could it be that our Lord at early moments in his life, for instance in the Temple and at his Baptism in the Jordan, had marked revelations of his divine sonship? On these he lived, and by constant prayer to the Father kept strengthening what was not given to him directly in his human experience. Father Bligh points to the fast in the desert as an occasion for him to reflect upon his divinity and his mission and to increase its vividness. Other occasions could be cited such as the Transfiguration: they would be intermittent and not continuous. That this is so is shown by Christ's joys and disappointments, the questions he asked, the surprises he met, the Agony in the Gardens, and the Cry on the Cross.

On this view Our Lord knew that he was the Son of God, not however, by direct experience; rather, it would be by a faith of the genre of that of St. Thomas after the Resurrection. Father Bligh brings evidence to support this view, some of which, such as the Temptation in the desert, has already been mentioned. He refers also to Christ's habit of praying to his Father before working some of his greatest miracles, and quotes Matthew 21 where Christ appears to say that his power to perform miracles comes from his faith. He deals with texts which look to weaken the evidence, texts several of which are in the Fourth Gospel, such as: "No one has ever seen God. . .only the Son has made him known," or "He who has sent me is with me: he has not left me alone. . ." and "I am the one who bears witness to myself." Father Bligh claims that these texts are not decisive one way or the other. Though I think they fit in here easily with a view I will give later, they can also be reconciled with the experience of one who has had revealed to him his divine sonship and who keeps that indirect knowledge alive by constant prayer and reflection.

Here then are two views, one of which tries to provide a psychological groundwork which allows for the possibility of a human conscious being aware of a divine personality: while the other draws evidence from the Gospel texts for a presence in Our Lord of a special kind of faith in his own divinity, strengthened intermittently by revelations. With the help of both these theories we can draw, let us hope, a little closer to the "burning bush," the mystery of Christ. We know from the Creeds that Jesus Christ was both God and Man, with two natures, therefore, and one person. How this union can exist and operate is a mystery, the full explanation of which is bound to surpass human understanding. Theologians with some reason have been concerned mainly to safeguard each single nature. They tell us that the human finite nature is related to the divine, whereas the divine has no real relation with the finite. This view has been held as being the only one compatible with the doctrine of the divine immutability. *

What we know for certain is that our Lord, though God, had a complete human nature made up of soul and body and identical with ours except in being sinless. We address him, however, correctly as God because instead of a human personality, the human nature belongs to the Son of God. St. John epitomizes this in the words: "The word was made flesh" and St. Paul gives a dramatic description of the mystery in his letter to the Philippians. "His nature is, from the first divine, and he thought it no usurpation to claim the rank of Godhead;" he is teaching a lesson of humility to his readers "but he emptied himself and took the nature of a servant, fashioned in the likeness of man. . .and lowered his own dignity and accepted an obedience which brought him to death" (Phil.2 6-9). Taken straightforwardly these words mean that the Son of God laid aside or stripped himself of his divine prerogatives in order to live as a fellow human being of ours and submit himself even to death. Now we know that the knowledge of Christ in his divine existence is identical with that of his Father. Becoming man, if he really becomes a man, this knowledge is laid aside. The evidence in the Gospels is there to show that this did happen, because Christ is always distinguishing between his will and knowledge and those of his Father. All that remains

Note Later I challenge this view. V. Ch. God's Immutability pp. 81-92.

then is his filial relation, and as the relationships of the Holy Trinity subsist by love, love alone remains in the new human life he assumed.

Now do we know enough about our own human necessities in thinking and acting to venture any farther? Rahner says "Yes," and he tries to describe a kind of knowledge which every human subject has, a subjective knowledge distinct from that which is always objectivized. He calls it a formal horizon, a previous enveloping knowledge in which knowledge of particular objects may move. It is preconceptual and he says that by it we assume before reflection starts that we are spiritual and free. This enables us to see where and how a divine personality could work. If I understand Rahner aright he is trying to describe a radical deep- sounding presence to oneself, which constitutes and certifies our acting as a distinct, separate and authoritative being. One that is free, responsible and spiritual.

From now on, helped by this analysis of Rahner's I shall attempt to distinguish our strictly human reasoning from what the person contributes in order that it may open a small window into the mysterious behavior of one who was God as well as man. In us there is this final judgment seat of the self, which is engaged not only in acclaiming what is true and what is false, what is good and what is bad, but also in authenticating itself and acting as an author with all the requisites to be more and more itself. This is indescribable in terms of our ordinary subject and object thinking. We see it at work in each of us in being ourselves. Contact with what is not the self, the not-I, pulls a trigger which makes us jump into self-realization. All have experienced the spontaneous reaction to an alien presence. We can dream our fancy meetings with other persons, with saints, with God, but let us suddenly become aware that we are not alone, that there is some one, perhaps a ghost or a thief in the room; then our own "I" becomes extremely awake. So it is that by the presence of a non-I we realize the existence of our own "I."

Nevertheless this "I" of ours remains strangely indistinct if we try to peer at it. It is like quicksilver, indefinite but potential. It is paradoxically half a mystery to ourselves, though we accept it as the very generator of all we are, what in fact prevents us from being anybody else. As we change, it changes too, and yet must also in some way be unchanging, the same "I" who as a child cried itself to sleep, ran into trouble, shirked work and discovered its own low rating, on reaching manhood. How much a part this "I" is of the world around it, once it is born, Merleau-Ponty has shown us. He has been most successful in making it publicly known how instinctively adjusted are all our baby movements to the world around us, how swiftly we familiarize ourselves with the world of time and space and human relationships. He attributes this with some truth to our body being already a piece of the world we come to know; it is a being-in-this-world. "I come into this world," he writes, "bringing my sensory fields and my perceptual field with me, in the last resort I bring a scheme of all possible being: a universal setting in relation to the world." Man operates in it long before he realizes what he is doing, and so suitably Merleau-Ponty makes use of Husserl's description of human intentional activity as the logos of the world of sensible experience, an art, he goes on to say "hidden in the depths of the human soul."

In Merleau-Ponty's account too much is left to the body. It is good to show the value of the body as letting us in by its being physical to share in the world around us. The quotation from Husserl gives the dimension of spirit, and it is essential to remind ourselves that what the body does for us in the physical world, the "I" does in the spiritual world. It introduces us into the world of truth, goodness and beauty and makes us at home there. Indeed the "I" can be translated by the word freedom, if we understand by that word the activity which is always making things it own and writing its own name upon them. By being free the "I" is in the world but also outside it; it is what Merleau-Ponty calls an ek-stase — a useful description because it reveals the double role of the "I." It is both subject and object, nature and what each person freely does with his nature. The "I" which is before us is an object, what I refer to as "me," is the same and not the same as the "I" who makes the reference. The "me" or self before the mind is a phenomenal self, something made up, my mask or image or what I really am. It is the "I" of the ek-stase which does the making up and is the final arbiter of what I am and shall be. This is the person, the subject who can never relinquish his responsibility with regard to himself, for he grows more himself by his own free choice. Now our Lord being fully human would have grown in space and time and with the development of the brain increase in the ability to think as well as to imagine and memorize. His experience of those around him, of the past and present would increase in time.If there is any inter-relationship between body and mind, reasoning and development of the brain, emotion and the hypothalamus and the glands this must have happened. All this belongs to Christ's humanity and its does not interfere with his divinity, because it is as subject, as person that he was and is God.

The "I" or personality, as we have seen, lies so to speak at the rear of consciousness, never itself the observed object as all else can be observed. We can never, so to say, turn off the light of the phenomenal vision of ourselves in order to see what we look like in the dark. The personality, however, has its own mode of communication; it does so by presence. We human beings do this by force of our free will and spirituality, which attest who and what we are, even as an author writes with authority and communicates himself through writing about something else. So our Lord would inevitably implicate his divinity in all he said and did. It lay, all the same, with our Lord to decide how far the divine authority and power showed themselves. At each moment of his life, divinity would be striking the minutes, stamping them into truth, beauty and love, but the degree of knowledge exercised would remain Christ's own secret.

Do we not, however, have a clue? In the Gospels we read of occasions when our Lord wishes to make a secret of his powers or withdraw them. But a clue to his general economy lies, I think, in those celebrated words of St. Paul to the Philippians already quoted. There the Son of God is said to have abdicated, by resigning his sovereign equality with the Father. He emptied himself, takes the nature of a servant and makes himself obedient unto death, a death upon a cross. Father Bligh argues that this emptying was not only of his glory but may be of his knowledge also. Now this would seem to follow from the emphasis laid on Our Lord's becoming a servant and being obedient. The language here is of course anthropomorphic but I think it contains a clue wherewith we can draw nearer to the mystery of divine love and have an insight into the life of the Holy Trinity. We can say almost nothing a priori of what limitations were entailed by the hypostatic union

But if we look at it in the light of the personal loving whereby the Holy Trinity subsists, then we can ask whether the son of God did not choose to set aside his own divine knowledge in order to be completely at the will of his Father — the instrument of the Father's plan for bringing man back from sin into the divine order. If this be so, then it is love which governs all and makes Our Lord have *nothing else in mind* save obedience to whatever the Father would ask of him, even if it was to be a death upon a cross. He blacked out from his own mind all that concerned his mission, in what way it would be successful and how it would broaden out into the salvation of the whole world. He would be as obedient as Isaac to his father Abraham. Trust and obedience are the outstanding features of Christ's life as a human being before he is raised from the dead. What then are we to say of Christ's knowledge? What we have said about the part played in a human being by the person ought *mutatis mutandis* to hold true in the case where a divine personality takes the place of a human one. The author of his work knows himself in his work; a person who is free and responsible has that unique form of knowing given by presence and authority. In Christ divinity, we have said, stamped all his behavior. It follows then that to some extent Christ must have been aware of his divinity because the personality of God was signing and authenticating all that the human nature did. This does not contradict what has already been argued concerning the abdication by the Son of God of his coequal rights with the Father. He could be humanly aware of his divinity by the very operations of self-hood, the while he signed these operations with the ineffable name.

One, indeed, among many problems would be whether Christ could ever lose that human awareness of his divinity. There seems no obvious reason why it could not happen. Human persons can pass through spiritual crises in which they seem to lose the sense of their separate identity, and if this be so our Lord on the Cross may have endured this extremity. One might point to the simple fact that in deep sleep we are said to lose all awareness of ourselves, though we still remain persons. (Let others answer that, for I doubt whether there is ever a total loss of consciousness while we are alive.) It may not then be necessary to adopt Father Bligh's hypothesis; that our Lord came to a knowledge of his divinity as well as of his mission by divine revelations. That this sheer existential knowledge should have been amplified and heightened by constant intercourse and union with his Father is, however, natural and probable. Because of his will to live by loving obedience he would always be wanting to know his Father's wishes and how to conform to the vocation to which he was dedicated. This is the natural interpretation of the incident in the Temple when his mother and foster father lost him. They found him in among the teachers in the Temple listening and answering questions; and in answer to their query why he had behaved in this way, he replied: "Could you not tell that I must needs be about my Father's business?"*

All theological works and orthodox lovers of Christ have laid stress on his obedience, but they usually presuppose that from the beginning he knew with certainty all that was to happen to him. It was decreed by the will of his Father that he should be rejected and put to death. His life was wholly predetermined and foreseen. Now the mystery of Christ's divine nature must on no account be underestimated; nevertheless the freshness of Christ's humanity is surely diminished in this interpretation. The impression made upon us by the Evangelists is of one who began with high hopes and expectations. His longing to be accepted, to be loved, his joys and desolations, his affection for his own people, do not find their proper place in this picture. Instead all is pre-arranged, and our Lord makes the suitable fated movements and addresses which lead on to a death which cannot be avoided. This does not sound right; nor can it be a final assessment of the most human and attractive figure known to history. Moreover it dims the significance of the Old Testament, making of it a *lucus a non lucendo*. There we read the story of a

---

*vide also tne prayers before choosing the Apostles (Luke 6), for St. Peter (Luke 9), and for the Church (John 14).

people chosen out and set apart, favored and disciplined, punished for backsliding, cheered on by prophets who foresee a great and glorious day to come, preached at by others who threaten a dark and catastrophic event. Why should a people be prepared for some decisive moment in time, which will depend for good or evil upon their choice, and when the time comes, have no relevant choice? There could be no importance in their choice seeing that the result was already settled, a foregone conclusion. An alternative can make sense, an alternative which gives a cosmic significance to the history of the chosen people. This would be true of them, if on their choice the future of mankind was in some sense to hang, as in *Genesis* the first representatives of the human race are depicted as making a bad choice which affected the whole future history of mankind. The vital difference between the first and the second choice was that the first lay between good and evil, the second between modes of salvation, a paradisal or a suffering one, for salvation had been promised but not what form it should take. This alternative has the merit of throwing a great light upon God's dealings with Israel, making the last act into real drama, the confrontation of Jesus Christ and the leaders of the Chosen People. His reactions, also, in his meetings with the people as well as with the Pharisees read so lovingly human; graciousness, sympathy, loving kindness, disappointment and the sadness of Gethsemane are there. What otherwise is hard to understand, namely his preoccupation with the Jews, becomes intelligible. They are the people whose choice will affect all other peoples. Hence, even though he was to be the savior of mankind, he can tell the Syrophoenician woman, who appealed to him for help for her daughter, that he is not sent save to the sheep of Israel. Such was the will of his Father. His own people must be won over first. There can hardly be any doubt that he really hoped for success with them seeing that he could say with deep sadness: "Jerusalem, Jerusalem, which I would have gathered as the hen gathers its chicks under its wing, and thou has not known the time of thy visitation."

The immediate objection to such a view as this, and also to Father Bligh's theory of "faith," is that Christ on many occasions showed a superhuman knowledge, worked miracles of healing, read hearts and forgave sin. He prophesied the future, spoke of his own death and resurrection and often of the destruction of Jerusalem. Father Bligh points out in reply how often we are told that Christ prayed to his Father before performing a miracle and in one place appears to attribute his own power of working miracles to faith (Mt. 21-2). For my part, the explanation already given of how personality has a singular presential awareness and of its powers of freedom and spirituality and, in our Lord's case, of his divinity, I do not see any difficulty in his working miracles, for example, out of compassion or as signs. These are expressions of his free and living human nature. Where his principal work, however, is concerned he seeks out his Father's will, for that is the lot he has chosen, namely to be the obedient servant. We see examples of the first in his compassion for the widow of Naim and in his tenderness to Mary Magdalene, though here the miracle is primarily a sign. His attitude is made clear in his words to the Jews (Jn. 6, 37-39) "All that the Father giveth me shall come to me; and him that cometh to me, I will not cast out: because I came down from heaven, not to do my own will, but the will of him who sent me." It is in this same passage that we have a clue to the knowledge he shared with the Father and what he did not share, — as well as to his human knowledge drawn from learning and experience. He knows the general purposes of his Father's salvific will, — "Now this is the will of the Father who sent me. . .that every one who sees the son and believes in him, may have life everlasting." this divine rescue plan was written in his heart and had been designed in the Council Chamber of the Trinity. Therefore he knew it as he knew his own name. He was to be as Simeon foresaw destined to bring about the rise and fall of many. Being lifted up, he would draw all things to himself. Therefore he knew that he was to be in his human nature the medium between man and God. It may well be, as Father Bligh suggests, that a better and better understanding of his mission was revealed to him in prayer and on occasions such as the Transfiguration, when he saw the import of the Old Testament and learnt of his "exit" from this world. Moreover he was soaked in the writings of the Old Testament, we see how he drew his language about the future from its prophecies and apocalyptic writings. Their meaning was inspired by God himself, and therefore a language he easily recognized as his own, and used.

What also seems possible is a kind of infiltration into his human consciousness of his function as the maker and remaker of this finite world. St. Paul tells us quite definitely of his pre-eminent position as a real Demirge: "He is the true likeness of the God we cannot see: he is that first birth which precedes every act of creation. Yes, in him all creative things took their being heavenly and earthly ... They were all created through him and in him; he takes precedence of all and in him all subsist. (Col. 1, 15-16). Again "It is God's living design, centered in Christ, to give history its fulfillment by resuming everything in him, all that is in heaven, all that is on earth, summed up in him".* These and many other texts reveal to us that in a far more intimate and magisterial a way than we could ever have imagined, Christ is Lord of this world, and all is to be remade in him. How well our Lord's almost nonchalant exhibition of power over nature fits in with this! He muzzles (as the Greek word suggests) the waters and walks on them; he commands diseases and even death and he bids the false Prince of this world "Begone." His authorship gives him a better understanding of life and history than a poet of his poem. His might be called an architectonic consciousness. By a sort of anamnesis he could see the world's panorama and bear in mind that his Father intended him to restore it.

> * *Note: A common view of theologians connects the Incarnation with man's original sin. Had there been no sin, there would have been no Incarnation. Christ came to atone for man and save him. Duns Scotus proposed another view, and that has spread. It is in keeping with the Pauline assertion of Christ's central position in creation. Creation begins and ends with Christ, the Alpha and the Omega. In this theory man does not end with the perfection of man: though we can see directions towards an end. The end of man from the beginning was intended to be a sharing in the divine nature through Jesus Christ. For further light on this theory v. Essay on Religious Ethics pp 93-116.*

We are left, however, at the end, as must happen, only on the lower slopes of the divine mystery. How could it be otherwise when one single person is both God and man? The best approach is in terms of love and in trying to glimpse the relationship of the Son of man to his divine Father. I have suggested that the much quoted text of Philippians provides the best clue. In a loving act of homage the Son empties himself of all that made him co-equal with the Father, in order to bring mankind into the divine life of the Trinity. Love dictated the terms of the emptying. They involved the Son's becoming "a servant, fashioned in the likeness of man" and we may go on from this to infer that the only prerogative he kept was love. Not looking to himself he chose to learn all that was needed for his mission from the Father. His portion was to trust utterly and to accept completely the Father's will. Hence he waits upon that will and rejoices when his Father is well-pleased. He seeks guidance in all crises and keeps himself ever ready by prayer. He has handed over to the Father all that belongs to the working out of the plan for mankind's salvation. It is this chosen ignorance which makes him suffer humanly when his own loving intentions are thwarted: and it is not without desolation and anguish that he realizes finally that is by the cruel death of the Cross and apparent failure the Father's intention of the salvaging of the world is to be accomplished.

If this be so the Agony in the Garden becomes intensely human and appealing and the Cry on the Cross betrays the moment when Christ came closest to the experience of sin and the damnation of bitter loneliness that goes with it. Light is thrown on the difficult subject of the parousia, on the mission of the Paraclete, the Spirit of love and wisdom, and Jesus Christ is justified by showing a new and unexpected way to bliss by humility and obedience: for "that is why God has raised him to such a height, given him a name which is above every name, so that everything in heaven and on earth and under the earth must bend the knee before the name of Jesus, and every tongue must confess Jesus Christ as the Lord dwelling in the glory (now) of God the Father" (Phil. 2, 9-11).

THE IMMUTABILITY OF GOD

It is high time that the matter of God's immutability should be re-examined, and Karl Rahner does this provocatively; but though he breaks the shell, no chicken so far as I can see emerges. He leaves us with the cryptic saying: "God is immutable in Himself, but mutable in another." In the context of a Hegel and perhaps a Heidegger this might be informative, but if it is meant to be a new insight it is too cloudy. What needs doing is a clarification of the attribute immutable. Dom Illtyd is surely right in saying that the Christian, if not the religious consciousness, does regard God as in some sense changeless, and even a pragmatist like Schiller praises the analysis of it given by Aristotle. If we now have to rise above it, it remains as an essential groundwork. Aristotle was influenced by the problems his predecessors left with him. The Eleatics, for instance, and Heraclitus, and his one time master, Plato. They sought answers to the problems of Being and Becoming, Unity and Multiplicity, Identity and Change. Aristotle worked to an answer from his distinction of act and potency; he tried to show that motion and all forms of change fell below what is wholly active and fulfilled, that is, the perfection of being *energeia. Energeia* is the completely real, and the perfect example of it, God, must lack nothing, must never suffer change or be touched by imperfection. The divine life is one of uninterrupted *energeia*, the *energeia akineseos*. It is a life of complete happiness, for as he wrote in the Nicomachean Ethics: "If the nature of anything were simple, the *same* action would ever be the most pleasant to it. And this is the reason why God always enjoys a single and simple pleasure: for there is not only the kind of activity which is a motion, there is also one without motion, and pleasure is rather in this utter calm than in movement. Change of all things is sweet, as the poet says, because of a certain defect." (It is a pity that Aristotle did not ponder over this sentence from the poet Euripides.) Here then is a kind of protocol in introducing God to man. He has a changeless activity all his own, an eternal self-consciousness of perfect bliss.

Unattractive as this description can be made to look, St. Thomas and the generality of Scholastic thinkers have taken it to contain permanent truth. It must, nevertheless, be seen in its context of Greek philosophical thought, the Olympic gods and goddesses were confined to the people, which is strikingly different from the Hebrew and Biblical. The Bible tells us of an ineffable God, who was both personal and providential, transcendent and self-communicating. The Greek discovered the wonders of reason and crowned mind with divinity. He had no special word for person. The Christian consciousness grew to love *persons*, and feel more at home with them: God was personal, human beings were personal and free. This sense of personality has grown during the centuries, especially in the last two hundred years. We have, to use a modern phrase out of context, 'come of age' about the 'self' - who we are, and what we are not. The evidence for this is in the spate of books on psychology, biographies, autobiographies, plays and novels à la proust, Virginia Woolf and James Joyce. Babies now weep over their existentialist fate and wonder what kind of essentialism is to be theirs, which it will be popular to talk about and despise. In more serious circles Aristotle is criticized for his over-concern with forms and essence: human beings are individuals of a species, not persons. God is completely self-regarding, without interest in anything else. He is the infinite enlargement of Aristotle's ideal, magnanimous man of the *Ethics*, who is so superior and self-sufficient as to be indifferent to the praise or blame of others. God has no out-going relation; he is a final cause but not an efficient or creative one. St. Thomas Aquinas as a good Christian, supplied the creativity, and has much to say on God's providence, but he is hampered here, I think, by Aristotle's impersonal, metaphysical framework.

In fact, it looks as if there should have been here a parting of the ways, for the Greek idea of personality was immature, and as a consequence our idea of God's immutability has suffered. We can still start with Aristotle and keep his scales of perfection, but only on condition that we value personality properly. We have to keep in mind what kind of perfection belongs to a person as contrasted with a thing or form or mind. Language about plenitude of being and perfect activity has a perennial relevance but risks hiding the personal reality of God. Our finite minds tend, as history only too clearly proves, to lose contact with the living God and to get lost in abstraction. God is buried in the One or the Whole or the Absolute or the Ground of Being. We approach God in a roundabout way. We have to predicate of him attributes, which in our human experience, are irreconcilable in one person and then assert that they are indistinguishable in God - justice and mercy, omnipotence and freedom, immutability and loving care. No wonder, perhaps, that we have been content to stay with such an unsuitable idea of immutability for so long. Now however that we have learnt more about ourselves, we have a better instrument for penetrating a little further into the divine mystery. We keep our eyes on what we know of selfhood, its possibilities and the intimate relationship between person and person. Here, though it be outside the boundaries of philosophy proper, the revelation of God as three persons in one nature quickens our understanding.

There is for instance, a connection between what we now know about the need for a plurality of persons for there to be any person at all, and the revelation of the Holy Trinity which is a paradigm of this. Language, child psychology, and anthropology have killed the old idea of an individual starting out from his complete interior ego to discover his neighbor and a world not himself. Now Dom Illtyd Trethoven was right in claiming immutability to be a primary attribute of God. God cannot be less than himself in his supreme perfection. But has Aristotle or the traditional answer exhausted the idea of perfection, and may not our idea of perfection change somewhat when we consider the perfection of a person instead of a thing? A hint is already present in the Aristotelian and Thomist description of knowledge as *"quodammodo omnia,"* "all things in a certain way" - for as the mind is enriched by becoming what it is not itself, so the person becomes properly a person by reaching beyond himself and communicating with others. In *The Sickness Unto Death* (p. 146) Soren Kierkegaard wrote that what we mean by relationship within a human self is that "the self relates itself to its own self and in relating itself to its own self relates itself to another." The individual becomes alive and self-conscious in a human milieu, and has no personal life except in deed or thought with others, as Heidegger and Merleau-Ponty amongst others have insisted. The self is not a ghost in the machine, not a Cartesian ego trying to outdo St. Simeon Styleites on his pillar-top. For it is by differentiating ourselves from those around us that we become aware of our separate, privileged status, and it is only by going out of ourselves that we can feel the glory of loving and living personally. "Only amongst men does man become man" as Fichte said (Grundlage des Naturrechts, Vol.3, Werke, p.39.)

All this however may be dismissed as irrelevant because it deals with the finite, whereas God is infinite, and immutability belongs solely and rightly to him. But what is said of the finite person seems to be applicable to a person not because he is finite, but because he is a person. That is why we attribute personality to God: we can think of nothing higher or more lovable. The highest perfection in the supernatural as well as the natural order is charity, and the wider and more intense this "caritas," the more perfect is the person. Nothing, for example, shows the Christ-like greatness of St. Paul so clearly as his cry: "Who is hurt and I am not hurt? Who is scandalized and I am not aflame?" In contrast to one whose interests are narrow and self-centered - indeed with the Aristotelian God - we have here in St. Paul one whose interests embraced his community and his world. He was imitating and portraying the Christ (who had said to him when he was persecuting Christians: "Why dost thou persecute me?" that is, the Christ) who took on his shoulders the griefs and sins of all mankind. In turn it is Christ who signals out as characteristic of God his Fatherhood and that Providence which cares for the sparrow and counts the hairs of one's head. So truly do we know that these descriptions give us authentic news of God that we never would say openly that God remained unaffected by the sufferings of the poor, the sick, the mother of God, or Christ himself in his human nature. We speak a different language from that taught in the standard books of theology when we have to defend God against the accusation by the rationalists that God is indifferent to the lives and fortunes of the beings he himself brought into being.

For images and analogies of what God is like we should turn away from Aristotle to the noblest levels of human excellence. In the work of the artist we have a faint copy of divine creativeness. All can see that an artist loves his work as himself - it gives him glory. This kind of glory has its prototype in the Bible. There it is a concomitant of divine action or presence. Bach is in his St. Matthew Passion music,

Dante in the Divine Comedy. A person expresses himself in his art and lives it, as a saint expresses himself in his passion for others. We become what we love, which may be the truth Karl Rahner had in mind. For a lover to be detached is a limitation, not a mark of preeminence. A mother knows this, and Solomon knew in his famous judgment how a mother feels this. The inspired writers of the Bible tell us throughout of a God involved in the well-being of his chosen people, so involved in fact, that he sent his son, prepared even to let him die for love.

The same conclusion forces itself upon us if we make use of the terms *eros* and *agape*. Without wishing to tie these two forms of love to the precise meaning I gave them in the book, *The Mind and Heart of Love* I take them to represent a recognizable distinction within love. *Eros* describes the love of self, self-interest, self-realization - its end, beatitude. *Agape* is love for another for his or her sake. The one is centripetal, the other centrifugal. In our human experience a being who sought solely for his own perfection and managed to succeed in enjoying himself would not excite our unqualified admiration - much less our affection. Is the case of God different? Yes, according to the old answer, and for the reasons I have already stated. To put them again in one sentence: God is perfection and infinitely lovable, and therefore he loves himself infinitely and without distraction. This view has prevailed despite the Christian revelation that in God there is a circumincession of love, a plurality within unity that suggests that at its supreme level love is to be looked for in terms of persons and mutual giving. This appeal to Christian revelation is, I hope, permissible as filtering light onto the nature of God and his mode of relationship with creatures. It would appear that the *agape* between Father and Son and personified in the Holy Spirit can overflow into a creation, whose final end it is to be integrated into the life of God. This is surely the only possible interpretation of God's *agape* as expressed in the words: "Father I will that where I am, they also. . .may be with me: that they may see my glory which thou hast given me, because thou hast loved me before the *creation of the world*." (The love here is clearly his divine love.) This, too, is the theme of St. Paul, and it has been given a scientific dressing by Teilhard de Chardin in his conception of a cosmic Christ, the *Alpha* and the *Omega*.

Up to now theologians have kept the revealed doctrines of the Christian faith and what is called natural theology in separate compartments. All change, for instance, in Christ was attributed to his humanity: his divine nature remains changeless with at best a quasi-relation to all that is finite. It is this playing down of the divine *agape* drama which disturbed Professor Geach. The doctrine of the Trinity enables us to loosen the too tight conceptions of divine immutability by providing new possibilities. If the divine internal distinctions have their source and meaning in *agape*, may not a free Agape of such unique power make God also really concerned with man and his creation? What can prevent love which is of its nature a pure giving from embracing all finite loveliness? The love even of finite persons does not entail personal loss. It is the measure of our increase. If this be so with us, let us allow God to act like King

Cophetua with his beggar maid. Far be it from God to lose anything by loving condescension.

Further consideration of this can be found in our hard-won consciousness of the importance of freedom. In the standard explanations of God's freedom, the primary object of God's will is said to be his own essence; and therefore God loves himself necessarily. All else is free. He has no need to create, and he gains nothing by creating, for he is necessarily the same whether creatures exist or do not exist. This distinction between necessity and freedom in God has always been hard to understand and harder to maintain. A simple solution, if it will work, would be to have done with the word "necessity" when speaking of God. Omitting that word, then, we can have recourse to what is our chief human asset, namely freedom. This freedom, it is now realized, is the root characteristic of a person, what the poet Hopkins called an individual "pitch of being." Add the attribute of loving to a free person and we reach the highest grade of excellence we can conceive. In this ascension, freedom increases and necessity dwindles. Moreover, the language of loss and gain becomes more and more irrelevant. The lover does not seek his gain: he is all for the beloved. In God supreme freedom and love meet. Whereas human love for obvious reasons is always subject to some necessity, divine love suppresses necessity altogether, so that in God all is freedom. One must never ask what it is necessary for God to do: with him all is decided by love. Hence we do an injustice to the nature of love even in saying that God necessarily loves himself. Here again the New Testament helps us out. Christ called all men to a loving union with him, and when Philip asked whether he could see his Father, Christ replied, "He who sees me sees the Father." These words taken literally tell us more of the divine nature than any philosophy.

In the never ceasing effort of man throughout history to know God, there has been a constant oscillation between anthropomorphic ideas and abstract unifications or negations. The mystics have perhaps exploited what psychologists have called the oceanic feeling or experience, and in losing themselves in the transcendent they have given it impersonal names. The Christian mystics have shared this tendency to write of God as an "ocean of infinity" as "superessential being," but in cleaving to Christ they have kept the balance. It was customary within the old prevailing idea of immutability to think of God as an unchanging beacon of light, or a constant blaze, with human beings coming and going. Such ideas serve to keep at bay the temptation to think of God too humanly. At the same time we have to make use of human ideals, and here freedom and personality seem to be the safest of guides. They save us from regarding God as pure mind, *noesis noeseos* or as *energeia akineseos* or Absolute Spirit. They bring us back from the precipice of nothingness whether we may be drawn in a mystical trance. We underestimate the freedom in which God lives and has his being, and this freedom does not make a whit of difference to his immutability. No necessity of his nature can prevent him from loving his creation infinitely more than a Father or a Mother loves the first-born child. In the discussion in France after Karl Rahner had read his paper, P. Congar asked whether Rahner's view was not already there, in germ at least, in the doctrine of grace. Hardly so, in the usual exposition of grace as a finite quality. It may be, however, that the distinction between created and uncreated grace can be revised; it might then turn out that in the revealed doctrine of grace which is a pure favor of God to man, that we have a promissory note as well as a presence, assuring us of a real and unique love-relationship between God and man.

The problem is eased, I hope, by what I have written. A concluding word must be said on what is perhaps the most disconcerting aspect of the traditional view of God's immutability; It is God's apparent indifference to the distress of his world, its physical and spiritual anguish. Here the apparent absence of God cannot be condoned by an assurance of his real care and love. How, too, reconcile the bliss of heaven, the immutable calm of god and his saints with the despairing, heart-breaking cries of mankind?

A perceptive answer is at hand, that given by the well known Anglican philosopher and theologian Canon Eric Mascall. He asserts that God has a divine interest in man's welfare and that he is full of compassion for human sorrows; but such is the infinite bliss of the divine life that compassion can never reduce it. In his own words: "This compassion is infinitely surpassed by the beatitude which God enjoys in the interior fullness of his own divine life, which it therefore can neither augment nor diminish." That is to say that compassion and immutability are compatible in a divine personal being, though we do not clearly see how, no more than we can understand how wisdom, goodness, power, and justice and mercy and other perfections are all identical in God. To us there is a problem in the countless joys and woes, good and bad acts, of the millions and millions who have been born into this world: they are more numerous than the sands of the seashore, and yet we are told in the exquisite *Revelations of Divine Love* by Juliana of Norwich that the tiny hazel nut of the world would fall to "naught for littleness" were it not cherished in the infinity of God's love. God, moreover, in his infinity has not to wait on time to know of repentence after sin and joy after pain. Of this I see a slight analogy in what we feel watching a great play. Our emotions are stirred: we can weep tears and almost cry for joy, though we are aware that we are watching a play and not a real tragedy. God knows and has compassion with the present, but simultaneously he sees history from beginning to end. One can be confident that through the triumphant atonement of Christ, God sees the *culpa* as *felix* and the finale as one when, as St. John saw in vision, all tears will be wiped away, or as Milton wrote at the end of Samson Agonistes:

Nothing is here for tears, nothing to wail

. . . .

All is best. Things we oft doubt
What the unsearchable dispose
Of highest Wisdom brings about,
and ever best found in the close.

ON RELIGION AND ETHICS

Almost every subject of philosophy is pock-marked with quarrels and conflicting opinions, but ethics (perhaps because of its seeming relevance to human conduct and life) is the most conspicuous for this defect. Within the last hundred years we have suffered from such confusion of ideas that the ordinary student is quite at a loss to know what is the end of human life. Before the time of Kant the Greek ideal was the most current and it had naturally been set in relation, direct or indirect, with the Christian religion. Kant broke this tradition in pieces by dismissing as unworthy of spirit the hitherto prized ideal of human desire. He filled up the vacuum he had created with the motion of duty for its own sake and by what he called the categorical imperative. It will always be a point of dispute whether the Aristotelian ethics allow for duty or omits it. What is less disputable is the minor attention paid to it in the immediate predecessors of Kant and the consequent resetting of the whole structure of ethics. T. F. Green and Bradley tried to incorporate the new findings into their synthesis, but both, very Hegelian in sympathy, tried to play down the importance of this new concept. The social desiderata of the times also served to divert minds from the peculiar character of the new problem raised. Men like Bentham and Mill were more interested in providing happiness to the masses who had been so neglected, and in accordance with their philanthropy they pronounced in favor of pleasure or the greatest happiness of the greatest number as the cardinal aim of moral endeavor. From the beginning of the present century, however, a closer and more analytic study was given to the fundamental assumptions and ideas of morality, and conflict was joined on almost every moral issue. The analytic school sought to clarify and uphold a pure and undefiled idea of the good and the obligatory, ideas which were considered patent and underivative and sovereign once they had been properly exposed. On the other hand the anthropologists wished to explain all in terms of history and genesis, the medical experts in terms of bodily changes and glands, the economists in terms of the conventions or shifting values of economic society, and finally the psychiatrists in terms of the unconscious and its prevailing instincts.

The result of this has been to bring chaos into the world of moral beliefs. An inventory of the views of the young in the universities of America just before America entered the second war revealed the alarming fact that a great number doubted the validity of moral distinctions and were unwilling consequently to pass any judgment on the rights and wrongs of the war or the goodness or badness of the Nazi regime. The Machiavellian principle that an end advantageous to any party justified any means used in obtaining it has become widespread, and many when pressed fall back on the assumption that morals are relative and therefore the discussion of them is vain. It is only to be expected that with such views current morals should decline and that our civilization should be threatened. Moreover, if what already has been argued be true, it is also to be expected that with the abdication of what I have called *"animus"* in contrast with "anima" and the decay of intellectual convictions and doctrines, a wilder belief, originating from anima, now ruthless and bent on power, now herd-like and somnambulistic, should emerge. Nature abhors a vacuum, and human beings cannot live without some belief. The indifferent and the disillusioned will take the easy course and turn to pleasure and selfishness a pseudo-mysticism or drugs; the wide-awake and the adventurer will make the most of the twilight by black markets and acquisitiveness, while the more idealistic will enlist in the ranks of some new passionate crusade. There remain those espoused to duty. When Kant planted the standard of duty, he substituted for the old Christian philosophy of life a moral imperative. It has had great influence on the generations which have succeeded him, especially so long as the old philosophy survived to support it in the rear. But when the old philosophy was forgotten duty was left high and dry. It has continued to make its austere appeal and it has had eminent followers, but events seem to have proved that morals, philosophy and religious doctrine have an intimate connection, and that each suffers when separated from the others. A man confronted with the demand of conscience is bound to ask why what may be in itself inherently rational is at the same time consistent with the general ends of life, and if his question receive no

answer or only one of determinism or vague progres-
siveness, he is tempted to ignore conscience or deny
its claims. This problem, Lord Russell owns, has for
years troubled him. In the past, however distinct the
ends of religion and ethics may be, the two have
always had contact with one another. It will be of
service to show how in the Christian religion the two
have interacted.

Fortunately this task has been made easy by
Henri de Lubac's magisterial work, *Surnaturel, Etudes
Historiques.* In the development of ethics the theories
of Plato and Aristotle are of capital importance.
Those, however, of Plato have a religious tone which
is absent from Aristotle.

The two of them have done more than any
others to form western civilization, and that influence
has abided despite revolutions and cataclysms in education and character-formation. One of our foremost
educationalists, Sir Richard Livingstone, continually
harked back to the teaching of the two great Greek
thinkers. Having, for instance, asserted that "in
judging any individual or nation, the most searching
question that can be asked is: Whom has he taken for
a master and how faithful is his service?," he gives the
truly Aristotelian answer: "We might accept excellence as master." Excellence is one of the translations
of the favorite word of Aristotle, *arete.* The argument
in the Nicomachean Ethics looks deceptively simple.
All should live according to *arete.* With our Christian
preconceptions and heritage we have become accus-
tomed to translating and thinking of *arete* as virtue.
Excellence is, however, a more accurate translation.
Aristotle starts off by laying down that every being

acts for some end or purpose. Nature does not act in vain, and meaningless action is inconceivable. As a biologist he noticed, as he thought, that the organs of animals and human beings had a function, and that when they performed their function perfectly they had satisfied and accomplished their aim. This perfect functioning is the *arete* or excellence. Similarly in human society a tinker, tailor, soldier and sailor has each his function, and he achieves his proper excellence when he has done his job perfectly. But if this be so then there must be an excellence which is peculiar to man in distinction from other animals. This will be his well being and give him supreme happiness, *eudaimonia*. In what then will this *eudaimonia* consist? True to the Greek tradition Aristotle searches for it in the distinguishing mark of man, his reason; and by dividing this reason into the practical and the speculative, he is able to work out in the concrete and in considerable detail his picture of the perfect human being, the man who lives according to reason and enjoys *eudaimonia*.

Into the details of this there is no need to go, but there are some points in his more general theory which demand attention. By dividing reason into the practical and the speculative, Aristotle made a distinction which once drawn made a great appeal and proved of permanent value. In the practical order we have to act according to reason, and emotions and passions are controlled and ordered by use of a golden mean between extremes, for example, of fear and foolhardiness, anger and apathy; in this way conduct becomes rational and virtuous. In other words, the reason is the master, self-realization is made possible, but the ideal even in friendship remains egocentric. This ideal of the practical order is confined to everyday life, and the mainspring of city and state life. If then we consider this ideal without that of the speculative intellect, it comes to this: that we can enjoy a well-ordered and well-orchestrated life in the company of our fellows, and this is *eudaimonia*. There will clearly be degrees of completeness, but at its best it keeps to a low and unambitious level. There are no dreams, no ecstasies, no supernal love. But this is not the whole story. The rational soul of man is not merely the animating principle of the body. It has a function of its own, the contemplation of truth, of the immaterial and the abiding. To Plato this side of life counted for so much that he at times underrated the images and shadows of our temporal stay. Aristotle had been a disciple of Plato, and he was far too great a thinker to ignore or despise the world of spirit. But he seems to shrink from developing his thought upon it. He tells us, indeed, in brave words to play the immortal so far as we can, but we are left uncertain even of the relation of the *nous* to the human composite. Later the Arabian philosophers were to take him to mean that the individual is not immortal and shares only temporarily in the nous which subsists apart and everlastingly. Whatever the truth about this be, Aristotle is more concerned to extol the life of the philosopher and sage than to work out into a consistent whole the *eudaimonia* of the man happy in this life and the sage who thinks immortal things. The result is that there appear to be two forms of the happy life, both resting on the privileged position of the intellect, and neither is satisfactory by itself. A human, temporal, fairly harmonious life is only a second-best, while the life of the sage seems to starve the other activities which belong to a full human ideal. Finally both ideals are tinged with egoism.

Modern critics of Aristotle have objected against him that he assumed unjustifiably that the good life, the holy life, the dutiful life were all in the end one with the harmonious and happy one. They make a sharp distinction between these. Nevertheless Aristotle was but doing what all spontaneously do. We do not separate duty from all reward or felicity, and we take for granted that the nature of man has a final perfection, duty indicates the lines to it, and when it is reached the joy in virtue will be of the highest. Aristotle, therefore, is to be commended for conceiving of an end to human striving and working it out in terms of the various excellencies of our nature. In the centuries which succeeded Aristotle's death his views were altered and modified and adapted to Neo-Platonic and Stoic ideals, but the main positions which he had established remained sufficiently firm. The early Christians drew their inspirations from his gospel teaching, but they had inevitably to make contact with his ideas "prevalent" all around him.

They were however, more interested in *nous* and the higher aspirations of the soul than they were in mundane morals. Hence they were more attracted to the Neo-Platonic theories of the good life than to the Ethics of Aristotle. But the distinction which Aristotle had made between the soul as the form of the body and controller of its passions and the noetic principle was gradually adopted. What they had to

say on this point is of great importance to the understanding of the history of Christian morals and ideals.
They did not doubt that a human being was one and
personal, but whereas one side of him belonged to
nature and was subject to its laws and movements,
the other side was of another world. The body belonged to the world of *naturalia,* the *mens* to the
world of *divina.* The favorite description of the latter
was in terms of image, and in consonance with Platonic phraseology the ideal was to change the soul
which was created in the image of God into a true
likeness. The theme thus developed, remained however, though often couched in Platonic language,
specifically Christian and independent. It sprang from
the Bible, from the words of Genesis, that man was
made in the image of God, and the theory, so to call
it, was a conflation of this text with the doctrine of
original sin and the restoring grace of Christ. In creating man God breathed into him the breath of life;
this breath is the divine *Pneuma* and as a reflection of
it the soul shares precariously in it. The soul, in fact,
is an airy nothing dependent for its being on love,
belonging to God and by that very being able to
respond to that love and become a divine similitude.

It must be observed that in this view there is
only one happiness for a human being, and that happiness is to be found in a state which is far beyond all
human conceiving or even striving. The Christian faith
from the beginning laid immense stress on the doctrine of grace; that is to say, it relied on the experience of love as between person, or soul and person,
more than on intellectual enjoyment, it thought that
God offered freely a union with Himself so close that

man could not of his own powers take even the first step towards realizing it. Nevertheless, this is the one and the only destiny for man which he wants or could enjoy. A *mens* or spirit could not be satisfied with anything else. There is therefore no natural end for man, only a supernatural one. This is utterly different from the doctrine of Aristotle, with his view of human nature as a complete closed universe, with its own powers and functions and its own excellence to be worked out in terms of interior self-realization and intellect. This latter is in Bergson's phrase a closed universe; the Christian ideal is an open one. Aristotle is thinking in terms of nature. The Christian ideal is best thought of in terms of love between persons and of a graced life. A person cannot possess another for his own satisfaction; he can only ask the other to give freely of his love, and it is the essence of love that it should be given freely. What then the soul desires is that it should belong to God entirely, but it knows that the finite can only ask this and not demand it, and that its own powers being impotent, all rests on God.

This view held the field for the first centuries, and the essential part of it, namely the dependence of man on grace, has never changed; it has reemerged in an extreme form in K. Barth. But from the thirteenth century onwards the Aristotelian doctrine began to come again into supremacy. Partly through the Arabian versions and influences and partly through the advent of new translations the very name of philosophy grew to be identified with the name of Aristotle. So much so that it would have been as unnatural for a thinker like St. Thomas Aquinas to ignore Aristotle as it would later be for a student to pay no attention to science. Confronted, therefore, with the philosopher par excellence, he, as it is supposed, baptized the pagan and made with the help of the Aristotelian metaphysical principles a synthesis known as Thomism, which is regarded by many as the most complete statement of a perennial philosophy. It is not the place to examine this generally accepted thesis except in so far as it bears on Greek ethics and religion. Up to the time of St. Thomas religion during the Christian dispensation had so affected moral ideas as to make them completely subservient to the supernatural end proposed in the Christian faith. And in doing this Christianity had succeeded in civilizing Europe and giving the arts and literature a new life. What then happened at the meeting of St. Thomas and Aristotle? If we consult the chief Catholic writers since the Reformation and look at the modern commentaries and text books, we shall find one, common, almost universally accepted interpretation of Thomism and one moral theory. According to this theory St. Thomas sharply separated the domains of natural ethics and grace. From Revelation we know that man is destined to a supernatural end, which is outside the capacities of human nature. This is a free gift in no sense due to man and can only be won with the help of grace. This therefore cannot be the natural end of man, nor can there be any natural desire for it. There is an Aristotelian formula that an end or good desired must correspond with a natural need and capacity. We can only want what seems or is to our good. It is because our body has a definite end that we desire refreshment; it does not and could not crave for a stone or for reading. St. Thomas, therefore, in accordance with these principles separated the natural and supernatural end of man.

What would be more convenient, then, to his purpose than the account of the natural end as proposed by Aristotle in the Nichomachean Ethics as illuminated by the theology of the Church? This great book then was taken over, its errors corrected, its inadequate conception of man's last end enlarged, and the part which dealt with *nous* transposed into definitive theological context. After the Renaissance the belief that this was the way St. Thomas had handled the matter became assured, and from then on a treatise on morals was inserted into the corpus of philosophy, a treatise which moved in the light of human reason, while amongst the volumes of dogmatic theology, whose first principle was supernatural faith, was placed the treatise on the supernatural end of man. In the exposition of morals the natural end was still *eudaimonia,* but this subjective happiness was coincident with the attainment of union with God by knowledge. In this way the beginning and the end of the Nicomachean Ethics were brought together and made to throw light one upon the other. The differentiating mark of man being the reason or intellect, the end of man must be sought in the highest possible fulfillment of his intellect's capacity. But this perfect life, as adumbrated by Aristotle at the end of his work, is to be found in wisdom and the contemplation of the most perfect object. Such an object clearly is God. Such was the reconciliation made, but it must be confessed that it was not complete. It still left obscure why happiness should be sought in one faculty and one faculty alone; it left over and unabsorbed into the theory the human moral life, to which Aristotle had devoted so much attention, and it left still more than a flavor of ego-centrism.

For more than two centuries this view seems to have satisfied a great number of thinkers, and it is still the most prevalent one. But controversy started and two serious difficulties came to the fore. The first was that St. Thomas time and again disdained to make the distinction which time and his followers had foisted on him. Frequently he says quite definitely that man has a natural desire for what had been set apart as the supernatural end. Secondly, it was found increasingly difficult to give a convincing picture of this natural beatitude. It must be such as to satisfy the highest capacities of human nature, to offer, that is, a felicity which all the noblest souls would recognize as fulfilling all that they could desire. Now for this the inter-mittent joys of our mortal life, lived amongst friends and enemies and with manifold duties, will not do. Besides no Christian, indeed, no Western religious thinker thought of this life as final; it is only the ante-room to eternity. But the joys of the next life are so obscure, save in so far as we learn of them in the supernatural order from the Revelation of God, that description of them has to be very vague. The differences of opinion among the theologians showed their hesitation and uncertainty. One, for instance, writes that natural happiness is to be defined by the natural processes and desires of our nature, and so we want to know the effects produced by God, in so far as He is the cause of them, the most universal, that is, and supreme cause. The distinguished Thomist, Bannez, writes that if we ask about our natural end, "I reply that it has to do with the author of nature and the giving of some reward to the immortal soul, and this must consist in the knowledge and contemplation of natural objects, but not in any clear vision of God." Sylvester Maurus, another Thomist, will speak of knowledge of God through creatures giving contentment to the soul, and Ripalda of "an abstract knowledge of God." These thinkers cannot get away from this abstract knowledge, though one speaks of aesthetic appreciation, and M. Peillaube confesses that to fulfill our aspirations, God no doubt will make himself known by means other than those of abstraction and reasoning, for instance, by the infusion of ideas."

I need not go into other examples to show how embarrassed even the Thomists have been to give a worthy idea of what this natural happiness could be. Perhaps the majority of them have been afraid of giving rein to their imagination and their dreams lest these dreams should come too near what in truth the supernatural end offers. Most of us probably have some dream world where love and knowledge and peace and beauty and friendship meet, glimpses of a happiness we can never make real and consistent to our heart's content. It was probably owing to meditation of this kind that a new train of thought was started some fifty years ago, and a slow conversion to another point of view took place. Maurice Blondel was one of those who helped to bring about the change. In his famous work, *L'Action,* he used a kind of dialectic to prove that, start with what desire or ideal one likes, one is forced by inner logic of that ideal through phase after phase of human aspiration until at the end one if forced either *vouloir indefiniment* or *vouloir l'infini*. Human hope and aspiration, if honest and logical, must perforce bring one to one's knees, if the alternative of proceeding indefinitely, like the Wandering Jew, on the same everlasting unsatisfactory level of broken hopes, is to be avoided. He pointed out how life was full of intimations but that this cause remained shadowy and incomplete, when viewed from this narrow angle of man's own self-realization, and in the meantime religion was becoming more and more emaciated where morality had lost its head and ceased to have any governing principle or objective end. Human morality and human ideals are of their nature transitory; they bid one adieu and pass one on to another whose embrace at its most poignant moment creates a new heartache. They are not the goal; they are but sign-posts. And if this be true, what is best in human life can thrive only when it is set in the context of religion and eternal life. In short, morality needs a transcendent religion to be its godparent. In the shining light of the Christian religion before the Renaissance all the sciences and arts grew together with theology as the mistress. The Renaissance brought many benefits, but it broke the unity, separating off into incommunicable sciences and sections the various forces of civilizations. A momentary self-sufficiency may be of great value to a man or movement, but isolation is in the end fatal to progress. Man began to suffer from a split personality, and the natural was cut off completely from the supernatural and morality from religion. Religion became emaciated, and morality lost its head and ceased to have any governing principles or clear objective.

The disunion and the impending chaos in social and national life have stirred nations to seek for some international federation of league and for charters which would lay down universal and concrete principles. The same desperate need exists in the world of thought, morality and religion. The new movement is to trace a closer connection between morality and religion, and in the Christian theology between the supernatural and the natural. Blondel was, I have suggested, one of those sensitive thinkers who heralded a new approach to the problem of the end of man. Successive thinkers pondered over this problem, and they endeavored to show that the highest aspirations of man, though they had to keep their distance from the supernatural and could not trespass or make demands on the free goodness of God, nevertheless dimly reached out to revelation and the happiness God has promised. Such a step was the first act of lèse majesté against the authority of the Nichomachean ethics. The autonomous character of natural morality was already threatened. The next step is interesting historically as well as in its bearing on the nature of ethics. It had become a commonplace that St. Thomas in baptizing Aristotle had taken over the Aristotelian view of ethics and distinguished it from the supernatural and given in the Christian revelation. It was therefore most disconcerting when new students of St. Thomas quoted a number of passages in which St. Thomas unequivocally wrote that man had a natural desire for the supernatural end, that every rational being was moved to seek the beatific vision. At first these statements were explained away, then on second thoughts they were made to fit into a theory which preserves both the natural and the supernatural end, and it has been reserved for the Père de Lubac to show that while St. Thomas made a totally successful synthesis of the early and traditional Christian doctrine and that of Aristotle he nevertheless maintained the religious and supernatural and as the only wholly true and complete answer to man's hopes and desires.

It is worth while rediscovering the true intentions of St. Thomas. In the first place he inherits the constant tradition of early Christianity which distinguished between *naturalia* and *divina,* confining to the former the closed natures of being below the level of reason and including the *nous* of man among the divina. It is in accordance with this tradition that he asserts constantly that the intellect can never receive its happiness save in the vision of God as he is in himself and in union with Him. But he also accepted the Aristotelian doctrine of nature and of every being having an end proportioned to its nature and its wants. The result is that the word *beatitudo* takes on various senses, which can be divided into three groups. The first corresponds with the poetic and significant distinction made by St. Augustine between *scientia vespertina et matutina,* evening and morning knowledge. The evening knowledge includes most forms of imperfect felicity, but its root is to be found in *De Genesi ad litteram* (1.4,n.40 *ad* 48. P.L. 34, 312-316), where St. Augustine says that evening knowledge is that which a spiritual being has by self-regard, and morning knowledge that which it gains in turning itself to God. In the first kind God himself is first known in the mind or self which knows; in the second, the mind or self knows itself better in God. The first is inferior and ego-centric, the second is all for God and through love. In the second use of the word beatitude, St. Thomas is concerned in distinguishing the joy which comes from the vision of God Himself from those which accompany it in the enjoyment of friends, the *gaudia socialia* of Bernard de Morlaix's *Caelestis Urbs*. His third use is an echo of Aristotle and by far the most frequent. Beatitude can be perfect or imperfect, natural or supernatural. By the imperfect is understood the degree of temporal or earthly happiness which man can attain; perfect happiness belongs to the celestial and everlasting. This distinction may for politeness sake be called Aristotelian, but it is dictated by Christian ideas. The present life of man is only the prelude to eternity, and the joys of it are only a beginning, an anticipation of what is to come. For this reason the happiness to be found in it is only imperfect. Nor is the nature of this joy of much interest to St. Thomas. How could it be when to the saintly Christian it was thought axiomatic that human joys were often treacherous and transient, and true wisdom consisted in taking up the Cross and in self-abnegation? But if we recall that in the thirteenth century a new civilization had come into being and that the makers had been Christians and were now faced with the problem of ordering aright the relations between the temporal and spiritual order, human society and the Church, we shall understand what lay behind this distinction of

St. Thomas. In the first centuries the interests of the Church had been almost exclusively spiritual; the Christians lived as aliens in a pagan society. But now a new society had been formed on Christian principles and doctrine and it behoved the theologians to give it a charter. This distinction of the two beatitudes immediately had its repercussions and became a shibboleth. We see it at work in the distinction of the two powers and in the disputes between the temporal sovereign and the spiritual authority, and it is responsible for the manner in which Dante, for instance, develops his argument in the *De Monarchia.* Seen in this light, the distinction has little to do with the Greek ideal of human self-realization, and still less to do with the later Thomist assumption of a natural happiness to be found in the life after death.

It cannot, therefore, be said that St. Thomas separated, as his later followers thought, morality from religion and the natural end of man from the supernatural. Nevertheless there is some ground for arguing that his views lent themselves to the divorce. This at any rate is the opinion of de Lubac. "It is true," he says, "that in transposing the traditional doctrine into Aristotelian terms he was more than any other responsible for giving rise to the fundamental objection he did not himself at the time perceive. For the "nature" to which he made reference, though spiritual, did not differ essentially from the other natures of which the universe was constituted. This was the nature of the philosophers, the one which the Ancients, who had no belief in God as a creator, had conceived." De Lubac goes on to say that this 'nature' remained that of these philosophers even though the notion was corrected by the introduction of the new idea of creation. It was quite different from the idea of the image of God of which the early Christian fathers, inspired by the Bible, had written. The relation between the spirit of man as image and the Creator was too intimate to allow these early thinkers to think of it as an independent nature. The implications of nature and image are too different. And yet, as de Lubac says: "Throughout the writings of St. Thomas the two conceptions of the Aristotelian nature and the patristic image are joined together, without it being clear how they really combine or conflict or which was to be considered primary. Vigorous as his spirit of synthesis is, he did not always succeed in moulding into a perfect unity the two elements which belonged to such different traditions. Looked at from this angle this great teacher, who usually impresses one most by the sturdy, if somewhat static, massiveness of his synthesis, appears rather as a pioneer and experimenter. His thought is still in unstable equilibrium which is the result of its very richness, and this explains how in time to come he could be interpreted in directly opposite senses." Those who took his expression, natural desire, in the Aristotelian sense, and thought of it as desire necessitated by our nature, could not in the end help separating such a desire from the end freely offered by God which surpassed all the exigencies and demands of a finite nature; and so in time they were forced to invent a natural end which would fulfill all the demands of nature, to invent, that is, a natural morality and a beatitude which owed nothing to supernatural religion.

111

The conclusion of de Lubac is that we must cut away all this dead wood of natural desires and natural ends, have done with the double end and the aristotelian nature. There can be only one end, an end desired wholeheartedly by man, though he knows that he has no power in himself to achieve it. Man must be thought of not as a nature but as a living image of the divine and as a person. As an image man depends radically and in every respect on the love which created him, and this divine love which, so to say, is in his bones, creates in him the longing for friendship with the highest. Such a friendship does not depend upon himself; he cannot demand it, though, as in all love, he will be utterly unhappy if it be denied him. As de Lubac very appositely says: "It would be contradictory to express the desire of man (for infinite happiness and communion with God) as exigence or demand ... It is at the antipodes to a right or demand; for it is essentially humble ... The I who aspires is not the I who makes a claim." The self knows only too well that it is asking for what it can never possess by its own powers; it is asking for what the other can only give of his own accord. There can be no necesssity in a pure love which exists between persons.

This solution, as given by de Lubac, has this advantage that it reunites religion and morality and removes what may be considered a number of false problems. There are, nevertheless, new problems which are in turn created by this view. Can we so easily remove from the landscape the idea of human nature as adumbrated by Aristotle, and if so what is left of natural morality and the directives called natural law and the intrinsic worth of a number of virtues, such as justice? I think that if we once more have recourse to the theory of two loves and the expression of them in *animus* and *anima,* these questions can be suitably answered. De Lubac in more than one place criticized the Aristotelian theory of nature's demands and fulfillment as possessive and egocentric. This criticism, if just, would dispose of its claims to be the last word on happiness and perfection. But on the other hand, the theory of the soul as an image has its own troubles. An image as such has no substance of its own; it is an image and nothing more. Now both sound philosophy and Christian theology agree in attributing a reality to human beings, and therefore in some sense to human nature.

At all times the leading moralists defend man as having rights and independence, and the Church in one of its most beautiful prayers addresses God in the words: "O thou who hast most wonderfully established human nature." Whatever then be the degree of dependence of man on the enduring act of creation by God, it will be an inadequate statement of man which leaves out of account altogether his intrinsic selfhood which enables him to respond freely to the destiny offered to him. Now the description in the word image does of itself give no hint of this intrinsic selfhood or substantial nature, and error can creep in if we press this metaphor too far. The truth surely should be in the use, if one pleases, of this metaphor to convey the belongingness of the soul to God, and the addition also of some other term to bring out the special status of man. If we turn to the two loves we shall find that this is precisely what they do. The *animus* is the rational expression of the possessive and self-realizing side of man, whereas the *anima* expresses its sense and desire that it belongs not to itself but to another. The egoistic impulse is the movement of the nature of essence to be for itself, of itself and by itself, and Aristotle, like many other Greek thinkers, was primarily interested in this "nature." The higher the nature the more does it tend to be an end in itself, and so we see in an ascending scale in the world of living things individually appearing, until at the level of man full individuality is reached, and men claim rights, freedom of judgment and will and a rational independence. Their special virtue lies in the activity of reason. It is as a rational animal that man learns to reverence truth, to respect himself and others and to have a legitimate pride. Without this self-respect no morality could endure, and no society could rise above the level of animals. Nevertheless this independence is more an aspiration than a reality. Society limits it, and still more in the face of divine love and power, it is necessarily subordinate to the other love. The Greek rationalist ethics puts a curb on the otherwise wild movement of *anima*. It stands for control, for direction, for the safeguarding of the sacrosanct nature of the individual man. But of itself it cannot do more than express vaguely the kind of ideal life which would give satisfaction, an ideal which is bound to be indefinite and somewhat bogus because it is egocentric and acquisitive.

Its value lies in prescribing what is really in the best interest of human nature: negatively through conscience which as Socrates realized acts as a monitor uttering "You must not. . ." when temptations come: positively as laying down two lines along which a human being can not only survive but reach his proper excellence. Such a form of goodness has to be articulated in laws, some of which will have fixed directive, while others will be dependent on circumstances and on the situation one has to meet. An excessive dependence on such moral thinking easily turns into casuistry and separates justice from love. It is only when associated with theism and religion that this autonomous system of morals takes on its full and far-reaching significance. Eros meets Agape and the two make one spirit.

In Christianity we have Agape fully revealed and so brilliant is its light in the teaching of the New Testament that it can blind scholars such as Anders Nygren to the presence also of Eros and the gospels. Agape and Eros are like mercy and justice which belong to each other. We cannot appreciate love if we have no regard for justice and so, too, we cannot understand love's exigencies unless we have a just idea of the splendor of natural human virtue and its ideal. Today we are drawn away from courts of justice to dream of a theology of morals where love is to supercede all rules and even to transform what is intrinsically wrong into a way of life. Such love is not the Agape of the gospels. It is more like the libertinism of the Dionysian Bacchant. It is founded on personal relationships beginning with the substantial unity of love of the Three Persons in one God and as all good things descend from God so this Agape opens up vistas of loneliness undreamt of by Aristotle or even Plato. The old, however, is not lost and for us Eros and Agape — human self-realization and participation in the divinity — must be kept together and not suffer division. Hence it is that the two problems of self-love and self-giving, of man's need of a moral code, the search of true happiness and the bliss of self-giving are overcome, for man must have for a human excellence something to give to the Lord who emptied himself of his glory out of love for human creatures.

THE INFLUENCE OF RELIGION
ON SOCIETY AND THE INDIVIDUAL

It is often said that religion is one of the more intangible influences controlling our thoughts and emotions. I wish to say something on the role it has played and does play in the rise and decline of societies and in the life of the individual. That it has played a role throughout the long history of the human race must be admitted by all, for historical records and art reveal it as being the most dominating and formative influence in early societies. The Bible gives us the most familiar example of its influence on a race, but that story is paralleled by the history of India, Babylonia, Greece and Rome, Mexico and Peru, to choose names almost at random. Temples and statues confirm this; from afar off mariners could see the gold on the statue of Pallas Athene at Athens, and tribes met at the shrines of their gods to consolidate their unity and to renew their strength. The pilgrimages to Mecca and the passionate zeal of the Moslem, the clash of the Crusades and still later in the wars of religion, the part played by the Orthodox clergy in national affairs, and the inspiration of a Ghandi, bear witness to the continuing influence of religion.

These typical examples just quoted make another point immediately clear, namely, that religion has aroused such passion that evil and good alternate in its record to an extent which has made sundry writers fear and abominate its presence. *Tantum religio potuit suadere malorum.* Lucretius, and many others detested what they saw of religion, and the very strength of their detestation points to its potency. No doubt high-minded men may grow disgusted with what they feel to be religion's bigotry and its at times hard resistance to rational inquiries and discoveries. But such reasons do not fully explain the passionate debate for and against religion, which has always gone on. It is the endemic influence, the passion of hate and love which it excites that makes the Marxist interpretation of religion appear shallow. It is not just a sop for the unfortunate, an imaginary ideal to solace those who have no opportunity of benefiting from this world's goods. Religion ranks with sex in its power to set fire to the emotions and change man, and we must seek a partial explanation of this influence in the nature of man himself.

Some of the better descriptions of religion enable us to see the source of its enduring vitality and influence. Its common denominator, according to P. Sertillanges, lies in man's need to get into touch with that "mysterious reality, on which, so it is felt, our very personal life and the existence of the world around us depend." He goes on to say that we want to know it, to gain its protection and to find in it an end and happiness. The mixture of abstract and personal terms is here a little confusing, but owing to the transcendence and mysterious character of what is worshipped, the mixture is perhaps natural. Cicero, for instance, in a well known definition, writes of a divine power which encloses human life *(Virtus quaedam divina vitam humanam continet).* It turns mens' minds to images of the gods, and the thought of a providence. Not very different is what Joseph Maréchal says when he denies that we can have any intuition of the divine reality, but we perceive it in the very movement of our being towards its source. We experience God by absence and want. "As one who knows water by thirst, God is anticipated by us; we have a prophetic sense of him." Maréchal is not saying that God cannot be shown by the mind to exist. He is one who believes that reason is not powerless before the mysteries of God; but he is emphasizing, what all seem to emphasize, what P. Gratry, for instance, tells us, that "the source of our interest and our power of passing from the finite to the infinite lies in a sense of the divine. It is a call from the infinitely desirable and knowable, which is not a picture or thought or a felt state, but a disposition to act, to act on some primordial and metaphysical alliance of the soul with God, a dispostion which is presupposed in every rational and free act."

Otto's idea of the numinous partly fits in with this picture. So, too, does the almost existentialist language of Louis Lavalle, the French philosopher, that "God is the plenitude before which I am as nothing, and without which I would not exist nor feel my insufficiency." More outside the chorus, but worth citing because it includes features so far not mentioned, is the view of Whitehead. "Religion is a purifying force, an interior life, whose principal virtue is sincerity; it is a system of general truths, which transform our human condition and personality." Defective on many counts, this description does give an explanation of why religion is essential to human living whether in society or for the individual. When too he mentions solitude he brings to mind the primordial relation of the self and God and the sign of an Augustine to be united with God. Religion bears witness to the fact that man is profoundly aware that he cannot raise himself to the perfection which he seeks by pure human effort, even with the cooperative effort of mankind. There is an umbilical cord which ties him to God, there is a weakness in him which he can never totally overcome, and there is a bourne to which he moves, which promises a love far higher than his own.

If this be near to the truth, then so much is contained in religion that we are closing our eyes, if we classify it with that brood of fears which so often accompanies religion; I mean superstition, magic, animism, sorcery, serpent worship, the evil eye and voodoo. These are like the diseases to which the human body is liable, and its witch-doctors are what the quacks are to the medical profession and the Paracelsuses to the true scientist. They are still with us, though it is natural to find them more successful in times when reasonable explanations of natural phenomena could not be given. But even in primitive times there were, as Mercea Eliade and other anthropologists agree, signs of genuine religion. Beset by forces around them which they could not understand, with nature now friendly and now hostile, tribes lived a more communal life, and made of the divine idea a sectarian, protective deity. By the mask they could impersonate him and draw strength from him, and in the dance they could pass out of their weak condition into his immortal life. Eliade insists that the primitive believed in a paradisal state, in a day or moment which transcended time, and in the presence of the divine, especially at the center of the known world or in the city or on the mountain top. Whether this be true or not, it is undeniable that religion was the formative and dominating force, holding men together in a semi-mystical unity, and helping to the development of the individual conscience and consciousness.

With growing maturity the idea of God also became clearer and, as in India and in Greece, great literatures were born, and philosophy and religion went hand in hand. To understand, however, the lines followed by the great religions, something more must be said about man's spiritual anatomy. The distinction between the masculine and feminine dynamisms, the animus and the anima, present and operative in every individual, has a place here. The one is positively life-promoting, life-preserving. This is what Dr. Kurt Goldstein refers to in *The Organism,* when he writes that "an organism is governed by the tendency to actualize, as much as possible its individual capacities, its 'nature' in the world. . .This tendency. . .is the basic drive, by which the life of the organism is determined." The second dynamism, wrongly confined by Freud to a release from the tension in libido and to disintegration into the inorganic, lies behind the phenomena of the herd instinct, the sexual abandonment, self-sacrifice and ecstasy.

121

The second is strikingly manifested in many religious phenomena. In India, as Mr. Arthur Koestler has recently argued, Yoga is a "systematic conditioning of the body to conniving at its own destruction;" and again, "the dreamless trance sleep of samadhi is a homage to thanatos, — an exercise in death, while preparing for the final samadhi in which it is consumed." On the other hand, Zen Buddhism, he holds, while it uses techniques which should suppress self-consciousness or, to use its own language, while it seeks to throw itself over the precipice, is maneuvered by the masculine Japanese and subconsciously made an ally of enlightenment and enlivement. The old books said that

> *Misery only doth exist, no one miserable;*
> *No doer is there; naught save the deed is found;*
> *Nirvana is, but not the man who seeks it;*
> *The Path exists, but not the traveller on it;*
> *but it may well be that the dynamism of*
> *abandonment and death has*
> *been subtly exploited to increase the*
> *concentration of the warrior,*
> *the business man and the strong ruler.*

Be this as it may, much of the evidence from eastern writings, techniques and behavior point to the prevalence of this feminine dynamism. The self is in the way; it is an illusion, and only when it has been rubbed away will there come a light of fulfillment in some Overself or Cosmic Consciousness. If a religious conviction of this kind enters into the individual's consciousness and habit of mind, and is furthered by long tested techniques of self-denial, the whole attitude of man towards society and the individual will be affected. Individual life will be held cheap; crowds will be at the mercy of a strong ruler, and indifference will be manifested in the presence of difficult conditions of life. Others will deal with this aspect of religion, so I need not stay upon it. They will be able to evaluate the techniques used to condition the mind and prepare it for a form of suicide.

In the West the opposite dynamism has gained the upper hand. We watch for it in the struggle for existence, in all forms of growth and in the ambitions of every individual. It is synonymous with Aristotle's *physis,* that is to say, nature in its process of becoming something, and man developing his own perfection of mind and body. Its ideal is in the Apollo image, where perfection of bodily health and athletic form go together with right reason and self-control. It is at the opposite pole to the frenzy or ecstasy of a Dionysius. By itself it is indifferent to moral good, though we translate the Greek word for excellence by "virtue." The weak go down before the strong in the cut-throat competition, which this dynamism engenders. It breaks out in naked ambition or in enlightened self-interest; it can sanction mere power or turn to the high humanism of a Goethe. But whereas the feminine frenzy flows easily into religious cadres, its opposite tends to create its own form of living, and has by education and training brought the art of living under moral and religious ideals.

In the balance between these forces civilization prospers, and it is in this balance or tension that religion has a necessary function. When Whitehead said that it had a purifying power, and gave a framework to life by a system of truths and by transforming personality, he was describing this function. Undoubtedly if one of these two dynamisms gets the upper hand and adopts an Apolline or Dionysiac worship the results can be disastrous, for a culture passes into a sterile rationalism or a dark barbarism. Moreover, within a culture the religion even of a high kind can be enlisted to serve evil ends. Like the energy of matter misapplied, religious emotion has catastrophic effects. Some of the worst practices in history, human sacrifice, temple prostitution, suttee, are due to this untempered religious emotion. No wonder it has been equated with sex as the strongest of all the impulses of human nature. The writer of the *Crucifixion of Man* had his eyes on the horrors committed in the name of religion, and a Gibbon could make it responsible for the decline and fall of Rome. On the other hand a Dante could see in it the expression of the will of God, which makes for our peace.

It is not the place here to dwell upon the failures of religion, for it could not be so powerful a factor for good were it not also subject to perversions. When clothed and in its right mind it offers a philosophy of life, that is to say, a system of truths and an ideal which can transform personality. As stating unambiguously that man is no chance product of this earth and that he has a high destiny, it is the salt which gives savor to a civilization. Take away the truth about God and his providence, his love and what is taught of the beauty of personal relationship, and those emotions which are sublimated in religion, attach themselves to some false god or ideal, to race or national ascendency or to the dream of a classless society. The whole of life, its humdrum pleasantries and aims, its Newtonian grandeur, its mystery and ecstasies, are crushed into a program which soon bursts at the seams. The Christian religion, to take it as a paradigm, gives room for all that is human to grow and spread, and that is one reason why it has exercised such an influence in history. As Friedrich von Hugel argued, it allows for the exuberance of the senses and rejoices in their beauty; it stands for reason and the cool light of reason in science and philosophy, and finally, it encourages within the context of the other two, the imaginative and intuitive side of man, which carries him towards poetry and mysticism. Without these parts of man cooperating freely there comes a miscarriage of religion and of the culture. Pasternak, living in an atheistic society, bore witness to this. He was forced into exaggeration as he looked around, but what he says has more than a trickle of truth. History, he said, in *Doctor Zhivago,* centers round death, the mystery of it, with a view to overcoming it. Now Christianity has supplied the answer by its message of love and its two ideals of free personality and life as a sacrifice (the two dynamisms of self-realization and self-sacrifice). "The ancients had blood and beastliness and cruelty and pockmarked Caligulas, who had no idea of how inferior the system of slavery is. They had the boastful dead eternity of bronze monuments and marble colums. Only with the coming of Christ could man breathe freely."

That Pasternak is here unfair to many great men

and women who lived before Christianity was born we must all agree; but much can be excused a poet who lives among pockmarked Caligulas and watched the sweated labor. His mind went back to the beginnings of Christianity and to the force which religion had in early times. I have already touched on the all-penetrating influence of religion in primitive societies, and when Christianity came it had an effect similar to what Pasternak depicts. The world was sick with a long fever. It had struggled to free itself from the foreboding that death ended all and that man was a victim of fate. Christian doctrines did bring a new hope and a new sense of the prerogatives and destiny of the individual. Few too will deny that, however badly some of its representatives behaved, and however forbidding some of the later doctrines may be thought to be, it gave play to the development of the individual person and of a society in which the individual could work with others in justice and charity. Hospitals, universities and the charter of the Common Law were the creation of clerics, and slavery gradually died out as the ideals of freedom and fraternity sank into men's minds. What had been a closed universe became an open one, as a living God took the place of fate or necessity as the controlling power and providence.

It would be outside our scope to show at any length the influence of religious ideas on western society. It is to the point, however, to distinguish between its overall influence for many centuries and the curtailed influence it now exercises. Both societies and individuals are conditioned in many differing ways and degrees. Once religion occupied the most prominent position, but that is not so any longer, and man's activities are now so numerous and complicated that the simple life of religion led by a primitive is scarcely possible. We must distinguish what can be called the vague or clear world view or attitude human beings accept or adopt. A child is constantly subjected to a barrage of impressions, and has to come to terms with them, organically and mentally, and so it takes up an attitude and lives within a prearranged framework. This is its "world," a world vague in outline and emotionally enjoyed or feared or disliked. Each individual has his own milieu. A man may be an optimist or indifferent or skeptical almost without knowing it, and he settles down with his fate or providence. This outlook, however, need not be fixed. In early times it was usually religious. Secondly, the child comes to terms with the actual environment in which it lives, as all day long it is exposed to the influences of its parents, companions, the country in which it lives, and its language, traditions and food. We cannot help being the children of our time, separated in innumerable ways from those of past generations and countries. The emigré to the United States used to watch with mingled feelings the rapid Americanization of his children. This kind of conditioning has been increased in one way and lessened in another. The old caste or class distinctions have diminished, but in their stead have come the new outlooks of the white collar clerk, the professional gamester, the specialist in industry or logistics, the university professor, the engineering technician and the expert physicist. Each of these has his own conditioned way of seeing what is happening around him. None of these attitudes is pure and undefiled, and after a time the diffused attitude of a modern city and capitalist life creates disquiet, and the young are stirred to a partial revolt.

This leads to the third type of attitude, one which to some extent rests upon a person's own initiative or decision. It can be called the moment of decision or the taking on of a personal philosophy of life. All accepted standards and outlooks are liable to be revised, for there is a law of tedium and of diminishing returns. Even religion, when it rests its case on reason and good sense, has to expect this kind of revolt and should shape its policies accordingly, as Hans Sach advised the Meistersinger to do. But in our present age the appeal of religion, and some would say the danger, is in the unfortunate conditioning to which all the young have to submit. They feel like a Laocoon caught in the coils of a vast serpent. Knowledge and techniques have gone ahead too fast, and everything can now be done on such a vast scale that the individual sinks into insignificance. Only a Christian sentiment stands in the way of his enslavement or use as a perishable instrument. I need not dwell on the complicated machinery now of the state and industry, big business and bureaucracy. More frightening to those who have to face a long future is the intrusion into the formerly sacrosanct chamber of the human person, the supersession of specifically human work by machines, calculating cybernetic machines, and new techniques for measuring human intelligence and work. Still worse is the threat that citizens may lose their private life when instruments will read off what they are thinking, and new drugs so change their character that they may become unrecognizable and willing servants of those in charge of the state.

Dismayed by so much that is happening and the growing impersonality of human existence, many have reacted in a way which has come to be called by the general name of Existentialism. The existentialist takes seriously the old saying that there is nothing of which man is certain save death. This is the human predicament. Confronted with extinction a man asks why this should happen, and what is man that he should have such dreams and such disillusioning experience. He ponders whether there be any meaning in life, who he is and what he should be doing. The sensations which accompany this state of mind are anxiety, dread, nausea, loneliness and nostalgia. What increases the dread is the spectacle of so many who have lost their souls within living memory, the spectacle, that is, of the Hitler youth baying before their idol, the Fuhrer, of those entering the ovens of the concentration camps and the hordes who gather round those lustful for power or with quack remedies for the salvation of man.

It is in this crisis that religion finds again its entrance and its metier, after it has been ignored by a society too confident of its own strength and virtue. The condition diagnosed as existentialist is like that of the religious outcry in the psalms and in other religious writings. "What is man that thou art mindful of him?" "Out of the depths I have cried unto thee." Religion brings back the lost framework of life, and gives a meaning to confused voices sounding in the soul. As sense and reason and emotion and aspirations are brought together in one heading, confidence is restored not only in general but in the significance of individual achievement. Moreover, the specter of death vanishes. Here then should be the remedial effects of religion. I say remedial because a man does not so easily come to terms with life now as in primitive times. There are too many competing interests, too much business to do which cannot easily be translated into a religious context. That is why even among those who practice their religion assiduously and faithfully, religion looks to be but one factor in their outlook. They have to be saints before they can be said to see everything, as the primitive did, through the eyes of their faith. It begins as a decisive catalyst; it sets a new system of ideas going, but this falls short at first of the category I mentioned.

Like all the other factors distinguished above, religion helps to condition a society and the individual. It remains now to ask in what particular way and by what methods this conditioning is brought about. A partial answer has already been given in the statements about the life-giving quality of a faith which is reasonable and rich in aspiration. For proof of this one has only to look around and consider what faith and hope went into the making of so many fair monuments in the arts, philosophy, and in the levelling up of society. More relevant to the questions before us, however, will be the methods and means which, let us say, the Christian and in particular, the Catholic, Church has used to instill into its converts and adherents a knowledge and love of the God of the Christians. These methods are best seen in the education of the young and in the rules which are imposed upon the members of the Christian body. And here I am faced with a difficulty. There are many Christian denominations and they differ in no small degree on the subjects of their teachings and on the stresses used in the teaching. Obviously, when St. Bernard took a group of his young friends off to a solitary place in the mountains called Clairvaux and taught them there to think as far as possible only of divine things and to regard the world as a distraction in their prayers, he was treating them very differently from a nun teaching in a parish school in Chicago. Again, many of those who descend spiritually from the Reformers of the sixteenth century hold the belief that the human race was corrupted radically by Original Sin, whereas the Catholic teaching is that human nature has remained radically good, though it is no longer in proper concord with itself and is biased towards selfishness and sex. Overemphasis, too, can creep in and spoil the simple meaning of some doctrine, and we have with us always, let us remember, those who are puritanical by disposition and those who are easy- going and kindly in their judgments. The one teacher can turn God into a monster, while the other makes of him a good-natured parent.

An error in stress can be very costly and lead to an antipathy to all religion or to the psychiatrist's couch, and it has been claimed that much of the power exercised by the Calvinist and Catholic Churches comes from their paralyzing the minds of the young with warnings against sin and threats of the punishments of a wrathful God. Such kinds of teaching were perhaps more suited to a rougher age, when warriors did not care for namby-pamby gods, but must be the exception now. Authority is for the time being out of favor, and general opinion is against the punishment of the young. The Bible, nevertheless, offers abundant evidence of the need of keeping a true sense of God alive, and a true sense of God begins with awe and fear. *Initium sapientiae timor domini.* The attitude of the Christian Church is often misunderstood. It is possible to keep the balance between awe and love and joy, but they must all be present if one is to sup with God. Fear is but a subsidiary element in the Christian teaching which is after all a Gospel, that is to say, good news, tidings of great joy. True religion is an exclamation of joy at the liberation of the spirit and the promise of living at the top of one's bent in the presence of absolute love. So great is this treasure that it must not be lost, and at times drastic means are taken to prevent its being lost. Such means are adopted especially on behalf of those who are simple and weak, the children of the Gospel who must not be scandalized. Let us admit that to protect them, the Church at times may appear to disapprove of what is harmless to grownups. What is good in itself is not always opportune, as we have seen in our own day in the too rapid concession of complete democratic liberty to tribes still fonder of vengeance on their neighbor than of freedom.

The aim of the Christian religion is to produce free personalities, because only *persons* can worship in truth and love. Hence, if we look more closely at the methods followed in teaching, we shall find great stress laid on reason and the ability to think out for oneself what is worthwhile within the divine order of providence. The mind should be prepared to have an answer to the main questions which life raises and the will, too, should be disciplined to take the hard with the soft, the adventurous with the domestic. The soul is made acquainted with mystery, with the transcendent reality which by its infinite perfection measures and sets him in a position to understand his own status. A hero or demonic power has from time immemorial been one of the means of drawing the best out of the young; the legendary figure who so often stands in the mists behind the story of the beginnings of a city or a tribe or a family. The households gods, and Anchises and Aeneas meant so much to the Romans. To the Jews Abraham and Moses were sources of inspiration and hope; they led them to expect a still more wonderful hero in the Messiah. To the Christian Christ is an historical figure, a man, and more than a man or hero, because he is the logos, the wisdom of God, and the love which makes the stars. To walk in sight of such a being, to be taught to learn his ways and fall in love with him, cannot on any count be called a dangerous conditioning of the mind. It is more likely to liberate the mind and set it towards perfection.

But it may be said that Christian practice, while it can aim high, has also fallen very low, and there have been more than whispers of how the Jesuits, for instance, have tried to condition youth. There is indeed a fourth type of conditioning which is unscrupulous and deadly. We hear tales of it from those who suffered under Hitler and at the hands of Soviet officials. Enough is known about the methods to make the stories plausible, and there is natural fear that as more and more is discovered in the science of medicine, the easier it will be to depersonalize human individuals and substitute other characteristics for the familiar ones. There are many new arts of persuasion besides the customary ones of slanting history and advertising propaganda, new pressures on the nerves, new forms of persecution in the cell and drugs to turn the martyr into a compliant tool of a party or a dictator. Has not Catholic teaching descended to a kind of brainwashing at time, and have not the Jesuits even boasted that if a child of four is put into their hands they can make of him what they want? I can only say that such a boast would be a monstrously foolish one, seeing that so many of the products of Jesuit education have been moderately or immoderately critical of their teachers. If we look at the book on which are founded all the Jesuit methods and techniques, I mean the famous book of their Founder, Ignatius of Loyola, the Book of the *Exercises,* we shall see how baseless is this charge.

The *Exercises* come the nearest in Western Christendom to the techniques elaborated in the East. In the West the Rule of St. Benedict set the pattern of religious behavior among Catholic religious, and a host of spiritual books followed in the middle ages. It is hardly an exaggeration, however, to say that St. Ignatius started a more scientific training in the spiritual life, and the *Exercises* are as exact as a military handbook and as practical. No one, nevertheless, could say that they prescribe a conditioning of the mind or put undue pressure on the will. It may be that there is something common between the techniques of Yoga and Zen Buddhism and the conditioning of the totalitarian states, because both wish to change or do away with the individual. Even to say this is farfetched, because those who submit to these techniques in the East do so of their own free will and with a purpose. St. Ignatius does use what may be called stage properties to get his effects. When he asks the exercitant to meditate on sin and death he suggests that fasting and darkness may help the mind, but the whole end of these meditations and exercises is to produce a free choice unencumbered by lazy feelings and a sticky will. He begins by a consideration which is wholly rational and intended to be logically convincing, and most of the book is taken up with meditations on the splendors of Christ as an example and an inspiration. Let us admit that in the rules written for the Jesuits themselves obedience is preached as a virtue, and to an outsider some of the images used, such as that of a corpse or stick in the hand of a master, may sound extreme. They are not so, however, in the context of the whole rule, which is founded on love, and in view of the freely chosen vocation of the Jesuit to be ready to take up any duty which the greater glory of God demands.

A little later than St. Ignatius the two Spanish Carmelite mystics, St. Teresa and St. John of the Cross, explored more scientifically the higher regions of prayer. Most high religions have had their mystical paths, and a clear philosophy of ascent is to be found in the Neo-Platonic Plotinus as well as in the Hindu writings. St. John of the Cross, however, is detailed and exact, and in his teaching the senses first suffer a dark night, then conceptual thinking, until in the end there is left what another writer has called the fine point of the spirit. What here looks like a method for abrogating the self turns into an enthronement of it amid flames of love. Neither then in these Spanish mystics nor in the Ignatian exercises and rule is there loss of personality. Quite the opposite, and Von Hugel was surely right when he contrasted a mystic saint like Catherine of Genoa with a psychopathic case. The latter grows more and more narrow as interest in self fills the horizon of the patient's mind; the saint and the true mystic on the other hand, grow more and more generous in thought and feeling until his or her world is almost identical with that of mankind. "Who is hurt, and I am not hurt?" Moreover, there is evidence to show that the moral and the religious sense is so part and parcel of the personality that it cannot be successfully eradicated. Patients who have been hypnotized are, as a rule, obedient to the suggestions and orders given to them. If, however, an order runs counter to a deep moral conviction, resistance stiffens. The same has been known to happen to those who have been drugged, or have had pressure put upon their will. Though they may be beside themselves, they nevertheless balk at the attempt to rob them of their moral and religious values. Those who are bent on changing them have either to disguise what they are doing, or attack their convictions circuitously. The religious dye colors the whole person, as if the person were so constituted that its selfhood were in communication with God or enjoying some ultimate and radical relationship with God.

If this be so, then religion should not be ignored

in any debate on the meaning and basis of selfhood, and we should expect of religion to provide a clue on how to preserve the personality against the threatened invasion of it by forms of brain-washing and by drugs. A theologian or philosopher cannot take the place of the physician and psychiatrist; he can do little more than give the groundwork, and even here he is handicapped by the varieties of religions and their varying tenets. According to some there are no genuine persons to preserve. For this reason I shall confine myself to the Christian religion. But even here there are differences which affect our judgment on the character of the individual. Julian the Emperor and many Romans of the later Empire accused Christianity of failing in their national duties and of speeding the dissolution of the Empire owing to their preoccupation with another world. The accusation has been repeated, most eloquently, by Nietzsche in his diatribe against the servile mentality of Christians and their otherworldliness. Many of the early Christians, living during times of persecution and hoping for a quick end of the world, did pay little attention to the worldly life around them. Nevertheless, Christianity has always managed to combine an ideal of otherworldliness with a duty to use talents in earthly tasks and with a love for their neighbor. The Christian does not regard these differing purposes as contradictory; they provide that tension which makes for a full life and, by the meeting of challenges and the overcoming of resistances, leads to the advancement not only of the individual, but of society.

The philosophy behind this is that man is more than a living material organism. He stands on the horizon of two worlds; he sets before himself a spiritual ideal which has to be realized through his psycho-physical organism, and his part is to make reason control the feelings and passions and sublimate the lower desires and loves into a high human love, which has a kinship with the divine. Hence every individual is of great worth and unique. The West has so taken to heart this teaching that the value of the individual has served as the corner stone of social, legal and political betterment. At this moment, however, a great question mark has been raised in many minds by what is happening around us and by what is being prepared in the laboratory.

We all think that our minds and will operate on their own steam. Language bears this out as well as judgments on behavior in courts of law. But the psychiatrists have made some of the old claims for freedom dubious, and the modern empirical philosopher cannot find a place for the self in his system. Dr. Kurt Goldstein in *The Organism* gives us valuable information of the working of the organism as a whole and of the relative constancy of the organism. He maintains that, in spite of the many changes which a man's character may suffer, and the unfolding and decline in the course of the individual's life, a relative constancy is maintained. "If this were not the case, it would never be possible to talk about a definite organism as such. It would not be possible to talk about a definite organism at all." Here is something relatively unchanging in an individual, and Goldstein in another place admits willingly that "all creative activity originates from the living impulse of the organism to cope productively with the environment," and that "consciousness is prerequisite in order that productivity may find its manifestation. . .It is ultimately consciousness which determines direction." He clings, however, to the idea that it is an abstraction to think of consciousness plus organism. But how, we may ask, could an organism create standards which make it possible and permissible for that which organizes life to give up its life for an ideal?

Austin Farrer in his Gifford Lectures for 1957 examines the arguments for and against the existence of the self and of freedom. He points out that when I lift up my pen or think aloud of what I have written there is no good reason for supposing that in each of these action or steps the part played by the brain changes radically. The action is controlled by the brain, but the action is in the organ, in the hand or the mouth. This is the part of me which I am using, and I am conscious of what I intend in using it. When we are carrying out a project or intention we often improvise and go on without a prefigured or fixed plan, so that it is almost impossible to think of the intentional act as prefigured in the workings of the brain. Furthermore, in the higher forms of organization, there is present a real power to bewitch the lower forms. The small scale patterns are set to a new dance by larger scale patterns. Again, the activity of a given action pattern and the transition from one action pattern to another go beyond physical laws. What this comes to is that our intentional life calls the tune. The neural action-patterns themselves have no name of their own; they are identified only as physical patterns corresponding to ordinary human

139

actions. On the other hand, the action of our intention is independent of any purely physical theory. Minute physiological patterns go on without correlation with conscious human intentions, and conscious human intentions go on without correlation with nervous patterns. The regularities deploy themselves. The minute physical energies, of course, go on working regularly, and we should be grateful for this, for it would be a serious handicap if we could not acquire bodily habits, such as walking, talking and reading, and cease to worry about them.

So Farrer acknowledges that human beings are to some extent controlled by breeding, physical conditions, interest and superstition and prejudice. Such conditioning, however, leaves a margin of sheer aspiration which goes out towards the object of a creative choice, and it is this creative choice which makes for advances in estimates of value, and for a stretching of inculcated principles until they are virtually transformed. An electronic machine, for instance, may do wonders within definite limits, but it is not going to change its basis of action, repent its destructive mission and immolate itself by plunging into the bowels of a volcano.

Mr. P. F. Strawson in his valuable analysis of what we mean by *Individuals,* to some extent supports the argument of Farrer. We cannot avoid, he tells us, falling back upon the primitive idea of a person. Most empiricists limit the connotation of a person. We must say, for instance, that "*I* am bald; *I* am cold". . .as well as "I see a spider on the ceiling." Such facts explain why a subject of experience should pick out one body from others and give it a name.

Strawson insists, however, that this limitation of the meaning of a person will not do, for it does not explain why the experience should be ascribed to any subject at all; nor again, why the I or the subject of the reference *and* the corporeal features should be attributable to the same thing. That is to say, they fail to explain the use of the word "I," or how any word has the use which that word has. In other words, they have failed to explain the concept we have of a person.

The problem of the person will be brought out if we suppose, as many have done and still do, that the person is a kind of compound with two kinds of subjects, the one an ego or pure consciousness, the subject of experience, and the other a substance with corporeal attributes. But if we started from the very beginning with such an idea or picture, we could never arrive at this compound idea of a person. If the ego, the pure subject, came first, we could not think at all of other subjects of consciousness, each distinguishable and identifiable. We should be stuck with our own ego in an unescapable solipsism, that pit which the modern philosophical positivist knows he is always in danger of slipping into. We could never assign our experience as such to any subject except ourselves. Worse than that; we could not do it to ourselves, because we cannot identify ourselves without others. This means that the pure subject or ego cannot exist as a primary concept, on the strength of which we explain ourselves, others, or a person. The concept of a person* must be logically prior to that

* *Strawson means by a person, one who is both conscious and corporeal.*

of an individual consciousness. This latter may have a logically secondary existence, for we do speak of a dead person, a body, and we do speak of a disembodied person, which retained the logical benefit of individuality from having been a person.

I do not think that this analysis is quite complete, because it presupposes that we cannot go behind the ascription of person to what is subject-consciousness and body. It has the merit, however, of removing some prejudices about the meaning of a self and bringing together in the human self both mind and body. It is this notion of the self which is such a matter of concern at present, owing to the spiritual power over others which is increasingly being put into the power of our bosses. This sense of the self must be carefully distinguished from another sense which is becoming very common both in scientific journals and in ordinary language. In the latter sense person and personality mean little more than character, and so psychologists like Block and Petersen will entitle an article *"Some Personality Correlates of Confidence"* etc., and Janet A. Taylor writes on *"A Personality Scale of Manifest Anxiety."* Freud, too, has, as every one knows, his language of the ego and the superego, and Jung has a set of distinctions of his own, which nevertheless, it can be argued, imply a permanent, subsisting self, which is even an *anima naturaliter Christiana.*

Ever since Descartes' time there has been a tendency to treat the self as a mind in a machine; what Ryle called the Ghost in the Machine. This tendency goes back a long way before Descartes, perhaps because the presence of the spiritual side in us is so striking and secondly because it is so easy to form a picture of it as imprisoned in the body, or driving it, or half in love with and half despising the body. This Platonic and eastern fashion of thought is harder put to it to explain the incursions of medicine and pharmacology into what was regarded as strictly private to the spirit. In the Catholic religion, on the other hand, partly owing to the dissemination of the Aristotelian outlook, the discoveries of medicine and pharmacology cause little alarm. The theory of the intimate interaction of soul and body allows for such discoveries. If the soul be the form of the body, and a human being has to be defined in terms of his being essentially body as well as mind, what affects the body should affect the mind, and mind and brain should function together. The difficulty here is to justify the high estate of the soul and its relative independence of the body. It is harder, that is, to find a self, and a self which is not completely severed by its organic activities. Why, in fact, look for something beyond what the psychologists call the character?

The reason is that organic behavior does not of itself tell the whole story; it leaves over the mystery of the self, which is there in the precious individuality of each person we know and love, and it does not account for the heights of aspiration and the acts which make up the life which man most treasures. There is a relation always between spirit and body in this life, but this relation must allow for the aspirations of which man has shown himself to be capable. To clear the situation Farrer gives us an allegory from playing the violin. Violin music may be freely and personally produced. But it cannot exceed the capacities of the violin, and however competent the performer, the music will not remain unaffected if we loosen the strings equally. He will then lose pitch. Or unequally; he will then go out of tune. Or if we knock holes in the sound box, he will lose resonance. "At some point a degree of interference will have been reached such that he can reproduce no semblance of music. Just as some men go mad, and all of us die; though it be that God will raise us up and put instruments of a new music in our hands." Few are surprised to find that when they have a headache they cannot think well, and from the beginning of history men and women have seen the effect of wounds and diseases on mind and character. There is nothing new, therefore, in the information about drugs which can send men mad or condition them to docility. The Aristotelian type of answer accepts this situation. It has always thought the solution by a pineal gland to be ridiculous. The Aristotelian type has, however, many varieties. There are some philosophers who see high possibilities in the suggestion of Bergson that the brain is more a protective or economic instrument than a creative one. All day long we are bombarded with impressions, thousands and thousands of them impinging upon us as we encounter an ever varying reality. Were it not that, like a model secretarial machine, our brain were sorting out what is to the point and letting past only what we can control, we could never grow and have a flexible and ordered mind. Another image of the brain is that of a telephone exchange. Reality strikes upon our consciousness, but for us to be able to report it to our selves and docket it, we need the brain. It enables us to talk to ourselves to be not only conscious, but self-conscious. When the exchange breaks down, because of a blow or illness, we are still conscious, but unable to catch our thoughts and call them our own. The thought is there, as the dream which vanishes just as we awake, or as with the very old who cannot remember from one moment to another what they have said.

Still another view deserves mention to offset what is feared by some to be happening now; the coming of the era of the faceless man, what has been called a revolution in administration when the privileged faubourgeoisie in contemporary subtopias exercises a faceless and standardizing influence on an increasingly lulled and affluent proletariat. Is something worse than this to happen? Is a man as proud as Julius Caesar to become as gentle as a sucking dove and an Abraham Lincoln to reveal the habits of an Al Capone? Granted that there be the most intimate union between character and selfhood, must there not be some selfhood which is inviolable and continues in one stay all throughout the changes it may have to endure? A static, unchanging self is out of the question, but to even any kind of self the empirical psychologist may give short shrift. He may say that there is no need to invent such hypotheses, for all that happens in experience can be sufficiently examined without the addition of such a self.

One kind of answer to this lies in pointing to the fatal flaw in materializing the mind or the will. Mr. J.B.S. Haldane was quick to see this flaw. If the mind is determined by matter and not by truth, then whatever I say has no value as truth. To use Haldane's word: "In order to escape from this necessity of sawing away the branch on which I am sitting, so to speak, I am compelled to believe that mind is not wholly conditioned by matter." In fact, the operations of the mind cannot be put into the same category as matter; a nebular hypothesis and stars are not the same kind of material. The same landscape can be painted again and again and can be thought of by different people without anything happening to the landscape, just as the earth existed long before Plato or Aristotle thought that they understood something about its nature. Aristotle talked about species and genus and the relation between them, but never could a genus devour a species as a cat devours a mouse. Not all these operations, which we call mental, are the acts of someone or something, and the effect cannot be higher than the cause.

If we examine the nature of these operations of the spirit we shall see still more clearly that the presence of some acting and subsisting self is required. In every judgment, we make an assertion, and an assertion .which is more than a conclusion; it is an assent, and an assent means that we make what we are saying our own and commit ourselves and sometimes our future life to it. In the law courts we swear to tell the truth, and it is in its very essence a personal act, for which I am responsible. (In a more profound analysis it could be shown that there is contained in every statement an act of self-identification). Kant tried to reduce this assertion to a mere formal unity, but this is denied by the acclamation with which every original act or expression or work of art is greeted, and later recognized as ours. What is true of judging holds also for acting and deciding. Any analysis which omitted the very special way in which we make one of two or more alternatives our own, when anyone of those alternatives lay within our power, would be far from the mark. It is thus we grow and become ourselves and achieve the ideals we aspire to, and all the language we use in descriptions of this process involve the presence of a subsisting self. This may be called the existentialist self, the one which has, down below the ordinary anxieties of living and choosing, that of a concern with itself and the desire to continue to live. In a paper read before the Aristotelian Society Mr. P.T. Geath pointed out that there are statements in which the word "exist" is a real predicate. When Jacob in the Bible cried out: "Joseph is not and Simeon is not," it would be quite absurd to say that Jacob in uttering these words was not talking about Joseph and Simeon but about the use of their names. Moreover here the reference of a name admits of no time qualification; names are senseless.

The poet Gerard Hopkins, who was no mean philosopher, called the self a positive infinitesimal. He had an unusually vivid sense of himself both for what he was as a character and as a singular, subsisting being. In his note books this passage occurs: "I find myself both as man and as myself something most determined and distinctive, at pitch, more distinctive and higher pitched than anything else I can see; I find myself with my pleasures and aims, my powers and my experiences, my deserts and guilt, my shame and sense of beauty, my angers, hopes, fears, and all my fate, more important to myself than anything I see. And when I ask where does all this throng and stack of being, so rich, so distinctive, so important come from, nothing I see can answer me. And this whether I speak of human nature or of my individuality, my self being." Still more is this the truth in the experiences of the mind and self-consciousness: "When I consider my selfbeing, my consciousness and feeling of self, that taste of myself, of *I* and *me* above and in all things, which is more distinctive than the smell of walnutleaf or camphor, and is incommunicable by any means to another man. . .Nothing else in nature comes near this unspeakable stress of pitch, distinctiveness, and selving, this self- being of my own."

Hopkins explains this distinctive self-being as a kind of positive pitch which every self has from the beginning, a positive infinitesimal or will which has its own way and inclination. From the beginning it follows its own line, and this line cannot with certainty be predicted. This freedom of pitch is integrated always so as to make one being in experience with a nature determined by heredity and environment. This nature is the area of its activity, the stuff which it has to mould, the Sparta given to it which it must adorn. Such a self is present in time of sleep as of awakening, and even if its field of operation were changed by drugs, there would remain not only the same body, some similar memories and ideas, the same language but the subsisting active subject which makes sense of there being any change at all. The self preserves the identity, which normally is transparent to those who love the person. In small matters the signature tune may be faint and recognized only by lovers and friends, or it may be as loud and distinguished as a Dante's or Shakespeare's, as determined as a Winston

Churchill's. In our liberty we are always creating and so becoming what we already might be, but of the many things we might be what we do become is the fruit of our liberty and very much our own. Such a self, while at home in the body and one with it is represented at its best in what is fresh and new and in the discovery of truths and in the choice of love. It is this self also which, as Mr. E.I. Watkin in the *Philosophy of Form* says, "has a radical orientation of the will towards eternity and the world of spirit- in the last analysis towards God, which is so distinct from the lower psychological impulses that it struggles to achieve freedom from their yoke."

There is a sense, then, in which the self can sustain many attacks upon it and continue always in being, in growth or decline, despite changes of the body, disease and a damage to the brain or conditioning of its dispositions by drugs. In his *Autobiography* the late Edwin Muir wrote: "I realized that immortality is not an idea or belief, but a state of being in which man keeps alive in himself his perception of the boundless union and freedom which he can faintly apprehend in time, though its consummation lies beyond time;" and again: "I think there must be a mind within our mind which cannot rest until it has worked out, even against our conscious will, the unresolved questions of our past; it brings intense contemplation." Put with this what Marion Chase recorded of her mentally ill patients. On being persuaded to try her therapeutic dances, they would sometimes cry out, "This is me." A nice puzzle is given to logician and psychologist by the remark made by an old woman who was off her head, when a friend came to visit her: "You should not have come, as I am out of my mind."

All images fail us in describing the complexity of the self which is fundamentally simple, for if we say that there is a self within a self, we are giving a false picture of a unique relation which has not even a far off counterpart. There is this self being, and it cannot have a true view of itself without an external world to keep it down to earth and others' criticism and idealism to improve standards. As one of the characters in Compton-Burnett's *Mother and Son* remarks: "You can do as you will with solitude. It does not take you on equal terms." Gilbert Chesterton said on one occasion: "a mirror is a wonderful thing, but not half so wonderful as a window." Some are called to live the life of vestal virgins, but too much solitude for most leads to idiocies, aberrations and misconceptions of one's nature. Only by contact with others and by living in the presence of those worthy of others' admiration can we change those two dynamisms which I have already mentioned, turning the centrifugal one into generosity and self-spending for others, and the centripetal one away from self-glorification and the lust for power, to self-respect, honor and integrity. In our fears of what may happen to us and those to follow us through the abuse of drugs and brainwashings, we forget not only that such fears have been shared in the past by those who thought of renaissance poisoners, of sorcery and evil eyes and love philtres, but also countless peoples have been in every generation slightly or seriously mistaken in their ideas about themselves. There will always be Don Quixotes, Malvolios and Peer Gynts.

Today the mask is a symbol of what people, who are uncertain of themselves, pretend to be. As Yeats wrote in 1909: "I think that all happiness depends upon the energy to assume the mask of some other self; that all joyous or creative life is a rebirth of something not oneself, something which has no memory and is created in a moment and perpetually renewed." Fortunately in the majority of cases we do not mistake ourselves so much as certain characteristics of ourselves. In judging who we are we act, to use another and a biblical image, like those who look at themselves in a mirror: "Like a man," as St. James says in his Epistle, "looking at his natural face in a mirror; for he looks at himself and goes away and presently forgets what kind of man he is." Even more commonly he sees a face which is not his at all, a face which is suited to his desires or is distorted by his fears.

The problem created by the transforming power of drugs is not entirely different from this problem of our true self and our quest to find ourselves and integrate our personality. The heart of the matter lies in our being able to go below the superficial impressions and standards we tend to live by, and in our being honest and truthful, steadfast and loving. Religion, perhaps, can help us here most of all. Socrates recognized that the true wisdom which so few possessed depended upon the precept: Know thyself. It is this kind of wisdom which the Christian religion lays down as the foundation of virtue and self-development, it says that without humility no progress can be made. Humility has been described as knowing the truth about ourselves and facing it.

Better perhaps, because the appeal to self-knowledge may seem to beg the question, is it to say that humility is the recognition of what we are in the light of and by comparison with the absolute standard of divine justice and love. The effect of this is seen in the *Confessions* of St. Augustine, and the inspiration in the saying of St. Paul that "I can do all things in him who strengtheneth me." The self abides *in conspectu Dei*.

ON CHRISTIAN JOY
JESU JOY OF MAN'S DESIRING

It is surprising to find how many times St. Paul tells his converts to rejoice. Clearly joy was an essential part of his teaching. It was to be the permanent lot of Christians. We have lived for so many centuries on Christian tradition that we have forgotten how privileged we have been and how dark the world appeared to those who were living at the time of Christ's advent. A French poet described the change: "a new and great hope has taken possession of the earth; in spite of ourselves we must raise our eyes to heaven." Human beings then seemed to count for so little in an uncaring world of fleeting joys, sorrow and death. And it was ever so. Men were as playthings in the hands of inexorable fate. The east and near east bear witness to this and the pagan literatures of Greece and Rome and Scandinavia. To take an example where a hero tries to make the best of fate: Philoctetes in the play of Sophocles is made to say on leaving his "sea-girt" isle: "Farewell, and may I have fair voyaging thither where great fate is leading me with the good will of friends and the decree of the Almighty who ordains all that is to be." Pathos here, but not the Pauline happiness.

The Revelation of a God who cares for the flowers of the field and counts the hairs of our heads, who has entered time to be one of us, washed sin away in his blood and promised a happy ending to sorrow and toil, created a new kind of joy. It assured the meanest individual that he was precious and important in the eyes of God with a special mission to fulfill before he was called to eternal bliss. This revelation transformed the listeners and produced that type of man which has characterized Christian civilization — the serf made free, the warrior turned knight and aware through God's love of them of their serviceableness and freedom.

The apostles started the tradition of Christian joy after the ascension of our Lord. One might have expected them to be desolate at his parting from them. Instead they were filled with the sense of glad tidings of joy to give to all the world. They hoped for Christ's return (not realizing that he was returning to them in his church) and they relied upon his promises. They were convinced that nothing could ultimately thwart such love as God had shown for mankind. Even death was swallowed up in victory. *Dux vitae mortuus, regnat vivus.* This sense of victory is part of the Christian character and to be discerned in every age. Pope John XXII, for example, at a time of disaster in the early Middle Ages had a Latin cuplet inscribed to the effect that though the world was falling into despair he disdained to be cast down.

The three theological virtues provide the basis for this interior joy which cannot be damped. Obviously even the saint is subject to many variations of gladness and sorrow. These are our human portions for "For who is hurt and I am not hurt." But pain and loss and wounding defeats cannot destroy that deep serenity of the Christian based on the truth, grasped by the simple and the learned alike that a living but invisible lord is on our side and with us. When St. Perpetua was groaning in childbirth shortly before she was to be sent into the arena to be devoured by lions, her jailer mocked her saying, "If you cannot bear this how will you bear the lions." Her answer was a perfect Christian prayer, "I suffer now but then Christ will suffer in me." The comfort of Christ is like that of a loved presence in another room of a house. To be without hope is to live in a deserted house but joy comes when there is a house and a loved presence. Rightly does the sacred writer describe faith as the substance, already with us, of things hoped for and the assurance or evidence of what is still unseen. Hope again lies in the recognition that he that is within one is greater than any forces without. Charity is the expression of Christ abiding within me: "I no longer live but Christ lives in me" in whom we say that all creation is warmed by the love of God.

These are the foundations of true joy. They are enlarged by our consciousness of the ever growing multitudes of true friends. Here are laughter and love of friends of whom we have so many, living and dead. The priest on coming to the alter at Mass kisses the stone where relics of centuries of our saints lie. They are our friends as are also the glorious band of saints down the ages among whom we have our favorites. And the Church, whatever passing failings it may display, is our mother. At times this joy is tinged with sorrow that many prove unfaithful to the promises of Christ or try to rend Christ's seemless robe.

Worldliness, too, can diminish our supernatural joy. The preoccupation with what is passing, with power and self-fulfillment can make us feel alone among skyscrapers and alien men. The old sense of faith begins to return and an impression of the meaninglessness of life. Man is an insignificant item in a blank, vast universe. Archibald MacLeish in a poem which appeared in the New York Times on Christmas Day, 1968 and was quoted by President Nixon in his inaugural address tried to raise our hopes by reflection on the amazing feat of the three astronauts who can now "see the earth as it truly is." The medieval notions put man at the center of everything, he tells us, and the scientific nuclear notion of the earth put him nowhere — lost in absurdity. This means, I think, that up till now man had been a "preposterous figure" or the degraded and degrading victim off at the margin of reality, and blind with blood. The past, therefore, has despite the evidence of Socrates, Plato, Jesus Christ, the Christian saints, and Thomas Aquinas, Dante, Shakespeare, Newton been a dreadful waste and only now "man may at least become himself." And the reason for this? We are able "to see the earth as it truly is small and blue and beautiful." We can see ourselves as "riders on the earth together" and somehow for the first time we are brothers who know now they are truly brothers.

The leap from the sight from far-off space of the earth as "small and blue and beautiful" to the supposedly "new" ideal of man as brothers seems a conclusion not justifiable even in a fairytale. We can truly admire the genius of man that can make such a flight possible and such a new sight of the earth credible. It is this which gives such preeminence, so far as we know, to man in creation — a preeminence already realized in the Psalms of the Bible. But only God in his love can bring men together as brothers prepared for peace through self-sacrifice. There is no genuine hope which can be based on knowing the color and size of the earth. Unfortunately, much of our scientific work backed by philosophy tends to make men into cyphers. The computer is ousting man, the State is reducing him, and he is losing his very name and personality in the mass production and business of the world. Several of the most striking plays of our time are concerned with the loss of the individual's identity. The growing dissatisfaction of youth, the vain attempts to find a new kind of joy in a lotus-land or a mysticism created by drugs are not symptoms of contentment or joy. They expose a condition of unhappiness which has been in no way relieved.

Henry James, when asked by a woman "What is life?" answered that it is "the predicament which precedes death." Death to many is the fatal enemy of hope. It can be made painless, but the grave does not give up its dead. Anxiety and melancholy are the parasites of death. The Christian, however, has an anodyne. He sees death not as an end but as a beginning." O death, where is thy sting? O death where is thy victory?" How could it bring all to a stop when he who is the giver of life dwells with us now in faith and hope and prepares us for the marriage feast in heaven?